AS OLD AS LIFE ITSELF . . .

In America, we celebrate the birth of a child with a baby shower and a christening or baptism. But America is a young country. Anthropologists and archaeologists believe Africa is the birthplace of humanity. As African-Americans, we are part of something new and something as old as life itself. To this new land we bring a heritage possessed of some of mankind's oldest traditions and customs.

—from *Pride & Joy*

Pride & Joy

~

African-American
Baby Celebrations

Janice Robinson

Photographs by Paul Shepherd
Illustrations by Katy Blander

Foreword by
Dr. Alvin Poussaint

POCKET BOOKS
New York   London   Toronto   Sydney   Singapore

An *Original* Publication of POCKET BOOKS

 POCKET BOOKS, a division of Simon & Schuster, Inc.
1230 Avenue of the Americas, New York, NY 10020

Copyright © 2001 by Janice Robinson

Library of Congress Cataloging-in-Publication Data

Robinson, Janice, 1966–
    Pride & joy : African-American baby celebrations / Janice Robinson; photographs by
  Paul Shepherd ; illustrations by Katy Blander ; foreword by Alvin Poussaint
      p. cm.
    Includes bibliographical references and index.
    ISBN 0-7434-0600-1
    1. Showers (Parties) 2. African American infants. I. Title: Pride and joy. II. Title.

  GV1472.7.S5 R63 2001
  792.3—dc21   00-069887

First Pocket Books trade paperback printing April 2001

10 9 8 7 6 5 4 3 2 1

POCKET and colophon are registered trademarks of Simon & Schuster, Inc.

Book design by Lisa Stokes
Photographs by Paul Shepherd
Illustrations by Katy Blander
Cover design by Anna Dorfman; photo credits: background, Eyewire; center, Bard Martin/The Image Bank

Printed in the U.S.A.

This book is dedicated to my three daughters, LaToya, Kristian, and Sessilee. Giving birth to the three of you has encouraged me to strive to thrive and not just survive. Mommy loves you.

Acknowledgments

*F*irst, I would like to thank my mother, Vernell Robinson, for supporting and believing in me as no one else has. My strength comes from you. I would also like to acknowledge my father, Bernard Robinson, for giving me the understanding that only the best is good enough. Inheriting my strength from my mother and self-confidence from my father gives me the desire to always go for the gold and to start from the top. In addition, I want to thank Veda Henderson, my best friend since second grade and unofficial adopted sister, for always being close by and cheering me on. I appreciate you being there. Kudos to my uncle Edell and my auntie Georgia Mae for helping to care for my children and encouraging me throughout my college years. Special thanks to the Clewiston crew in Harlem and my Pensacola peeps, also known as my family, who gave me my roots.

To my partner, Marta Sanchez-Speer, who compares our entrepreneurship to "fleas holding steadfast on to a bucking bull," thanks for hanging in there, baby! High regards to my editor, Tracy Sherrod, and her assistant, Calaya Reid, for walking me through this long process. Amy Einhorn, thanks for your special insight and assistance in structuring this book. To my hardworking agents, Barbara Lowenstein and Madeleine Morel, I am so glad you found me; I will be forever grateful. I am appreciative of Dr. Alvin Poussaint, of Judge Baker Children's Center at Harvard University, for writing the foreword to this book. Thanks go to Dr. Phillip L. Kilbride, of Bryn Mawr College, for allowing me the unlimited use of his office and library.

I am also indebted to Dr. Alma Gottlieb, of the University of Illinois, for her contributing research, and to Lisa Edwards, of E-Z Tours in New York, for a wonderful trip to Senegal and her African expertise. Thanks to Emily Gunther for her assistance with the spiritual shower. My sister-friend and diva, Jacquelyn Mooney, of Rhythm & Hues Quilts in New Orleans, your community-quilt contribution was superb. Many thanks to Gary and Lisa Shepherd for having their daddy shower right on time for this book. My sincerest appreciation to my most talented illustrator, Katy Blander, for your endless dedication and hard work. You helped to make my book look like "all that" (as my kids would say!). Last but definitely not least, my special recognition and love goes out to Paul Shepherd for his great talent, enthusiasm, and abundant creativity in photographing this book. To everyone I know, I am forever blessed by having you in my life.

Contents

Foreword by Dr. Alvin Poussaint   xiii

Introduction   xvii

PART I   SHOWERED WITH LOVE   1

1   The Afrocentric Baby Shower   3

2   Religious Elements   15

3   Food for Thought   21

4   Planning the Baby Shower   35

5   All Wrapped Up   67

PART II   BIRTH CUSTOMS AND RITUALS   81

6   The Birth of a New Child   83

PART III   THE NAMING CEREMONY   89

7   What's in a Name?   91

8   The Traditional Naming Ceremony   99

9   Preparations for the Naming Ceremony   103

10   The Naming Ceremony Rites   111

11   A Fabulous Feast   117

12   African Naming Ceremonies   125

13   Naming Ceremonies for Older Folks   129

X CONTENTS

PART IV   RESOURCE GUIDE   135

Appendix A: Afrocentric Patterns for Invitations, Decorations, and Party Favors   147

Appendix B: Popular Urban Names   149

Bibliography   179

Tell Us Your Story   181

Index   183

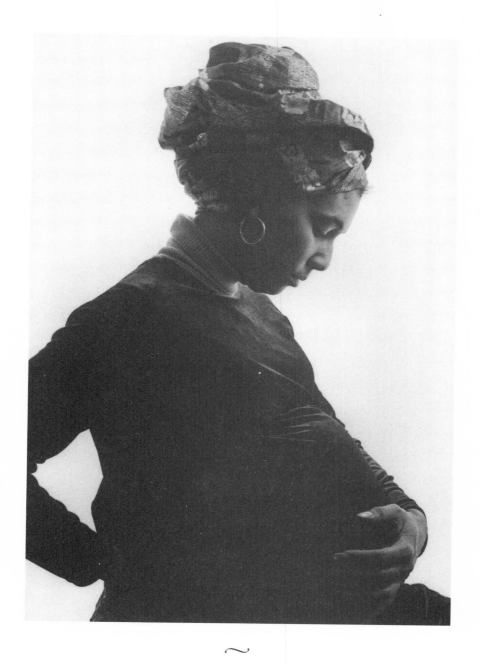

~

The child is yours alone while it is in the womb.
When it comes out, it is for everybody.

—Ibo proverb, Nigeria

Foreword

*H*istorically, African-American communities have treasured their infants. Relatives and friends have often been as important as parents to a child's well-being. In fact, it has been this tradition of kinship—the great strength of the African-American family—that has sustained both children and adults in the bleakest of times. It enabled many transplanted Africans to survive the horrors of enslavement. And it has helped African-Americans to keep on in the face of discrimination.

In recent decades, though, the powerful kinship bonds of African-American families have been weakened. Family members are more likely to live in different parts of the country than they are to live in different houses on the same street, and more than half of all African-American children now live in households headed by single mothers. As the twenty-first century begins, the disruption of the extended family is causing many African-Americans to experience a new sense of isolation. And although African-Americans historically have opened their arms to rejoice in the coming of a grandchild, niece, or god-child, seldom rejecting even so-called illegitimate children, we are seeing more reports of child abuse and neglect.

Pride & Joy, a collection of baby celebrations from African and other world cultures, thus comes as a timely reminder that every child is precious.

Having a baby in America is often an isolating experience, a medical event rather than a spiritual one. Mothers typically give birth in a sterile hospital setting, and although fathers are now welcome in many delivery rooms, and even expected to play an active role in their children's births, other relatives and

friends are usually excluded. When mother and baby are released from the hospital, the family is frequently on its own. Parents seldom go home to a close-knit community of relative and friends. Grandmothers no longer live just down the hall or across the street. Yet new parents typically feel they are not wise enough, not strong enough, not patient enough to care for a fragile newborn, and they often feel mild anxiety the first time they're left alone with their baby. Simply knowing they can rely on the help and experiences of others who have been there (and survived) can greatly boost their confidence as parents.

The new parent's need for support has long been recognized by most cultures. It has been expressed in countless maxims, from the familiar "It takes a village to raise a child" to the wise proverb of Nigeria's Ibo that author Janice Robinson retells:

The child is yours alone while it is in the womb. When it comes out, it is for everybody.

In making the childbirth celebrations of African and other world cultures available to readers, *Pride & Joy*'s most important contribution may well be the uplifting message it delivers: the birth of a child is a deeply spiritual event, and it is important for the entire community, not just the parents, to celebrate each birth.

Robinson notes that many African peoples believe birth and death are transitions between the spiritual and earthly worlds, and a baby is a gift from God, or Allah. And she offers heartening illustrations of communities gathering to support and encourage parents with their newborns. The ceremonies for celebrating a child's birth that *Pride & Joy* describes are rich in tradition and meaning. But what is even more important is that these ceremonies declare the partnership of parents and community.

Baby showers, a popular American tradition, can seem like nothing more than an excuse for people to get together for an hour or two and display expensive gifts. In contrast, the traditions Robinson describes have the deeper purpose of reinforcing our ties to each other, as her comment about a traditional African ritual makes clear:

This gesture of kindness and solidarity is designed to
remind the new mother that she may not now see where she is
going, but she is going to get there, even though she may
not know or see who will help her along the way. She
will come to realize that those whom she can see and those
whom she can't see will always be there for her.

Along with illustrating ceremonies to celebrate the birth of a child, Robinson devotes a section of the book to a related milestone, often glossed over in American culture, that has a particular significance for African-Americans: the naming of a child. Perhaps because slavery took the names away from Africans brought to this country, many of us now feel it is important to give our child a name that has a special meaning, sometimes one with African roots; often we will add a family name so that ancestors may not be forgotten. In recognition of the significance attached to selecting and bestowing a child's name, Robinson describes naming ceremonies that honor a child's individuality while reflecting the miracle each infant represents for the larger human family.

Finally, for readers who would like to celebrate the birth of a child in a way that reflects cultural awareness but who might find it difficult to import traditions from other peoples directly into their lives, there is room for modifying ceremonies. Robinson's practical suggestions are designed to help such households successfully incorporate traditions they particularly like.

Overall, Robinson's collection of traditions from around the world provides a rich assortment for African-American parents to sample, and readers are likely to find at least one celebration they will want to use as they mark the beginning of a great journey with their own bundle of pride and joy.

Alvin F. Poussaint, M.D.
Clinical Professor of Psychiatry,
Harvard Medical School and
Judge Baker Children's Center,
Boston, Massachusetts

Introduction

 ## PRIDE & JOY!

I decided to write this book while researching a *Successful Black Parenting* magazine article on hosting an Afrocentric baby shower. During my research, I discovered the ritual of African naming ceremonies for newborns and was intrigued by the inspiring symbolism behind the event. I thought the ceremony was a wonderful way to start off a new life, by celebrating the meaning behind the newborn and who that little person will one day become. I instantly contemplated the meaning of my own name. Though not African in origin, the name "Janice" means "God of Open Doors." My mother once told me that a nurse at my birth told her I "would never want for anything and doors would be opened for [me] throughout my life." I grew up

thinking there was nothing I couldn't accomplish. And as a child, it was kind of cool knowing that my name was that of a god. After I uncovered this ancient tradition, I wanted to share it with every African-American parent, so I took a trip to Africa to observe infant rituals personally.

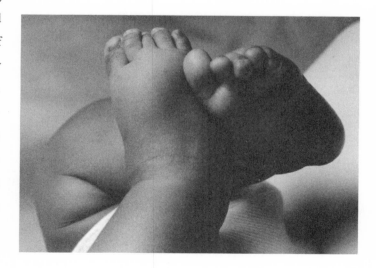

In the summer of 1997, I went to Senegal, in West Africa. My trip included observing infant naming ceremonies and rituals and participating in an adult naming ceremony for a group of Americans in a small village called Kounoune. The members of this group were strangers to the community; however, we were greeted as brothers and sisters and welcomed to our "true home." We were told that "a person cannot truly be called African-American until he or she has experienced Africa firsthand." We were also told that "America may be our house, but Africa is our home."

For this ceremony, all of the village children surrounded us in a circle while the drummers beat their drums. As we looked on in awe, the older women stood up in the sand and began dancing. Some of them looked as if they could be about ninety years old. They danced together, alone, and then with us. In Africa, it is customary for the women to dance before the men.

The older women then challenged the younger women in dance, by dancing faster to the increased tempo of the drum beat. The children were enthralled. We brought gifts for our namesakes who lived in the village, and we were given our new African names. The name I was given—my new Senegalese name—is Fatou Ngdoye. "Fatou" is a popular Senegalese name that means "beloved by all."

This was an incredible experience that I will never forget—a turning point in my life. Africans believe that a name can determine a person's destiny and change one's life. I believe the traditional African naming ceremony can do for your family and friends what it has done for me. It gave me new direction and great pride to know who I am, and it has inspired me to strive for excellence.

Having a baby is an exciting yet frightening period in any woman's life. This momentous event and rites of passage into motherhood should be celebrated appropriately, for nothing on earth can bring a woman, a family, a community, or a culture more pride and joy!

A Zairean proverb states, "Children are the reward of life." In Africa, people celebrate the birth of a child together. It is a festive event shared by the entire community. Dance and music commemorate each new addition to the village. In the movie *Roots*, there is a dramatic scene in which the infant Kunta Kinte is being offered to God by his father, who thrusts the child upward toward the heavens. "Behold the only thing greater than yourself," he tells his newborn son. African-American naming ceremonies and baby showers are rites of passage both for the parents and for their newborn child.

In America, we celebrate the birth of a child with a baby shower and a christening or baptism. But America is a young country. Anthropologists and archaeologists believe Africa is the birthplace of humanity. As African-Americans, we are a part of something new and something as old as life itself. To this new land we bring a heritage possessed of some of mankind's oldest traditions and customs.

When a sister, friend, or family member makes the commitment to host a baby shower, she is bringing together the community of the mom-to-be—whom I refer to as the mother-of-honor—to support her new family. The shower provides the expectant or new mother with an opportunity to begin the process of bonding herself and her child with the community, and to make the baby welcome in her world. Parents can make this event very memorable by incorporating elements of our great African heritage. This reflects and celebrates not only who we are but also who this new baby will become. These tried-and-true customs and traditions, which were taught to our ancestors thousands of years ago and carried through the ages, deserve to be re-created and passed on to each new generation. A baby shower with an African-American theme presents a perfect opportunity to introduce our magnificent heritage into the infant's life and to our community.

Naming ceremonies are similar to a christening or baptism, except here the purpose is to name the newborn and welcome the infant into the family and community. There are usually no godparents, who, in the Western tradition, are secondarily responsible for the child's spiritual well-being. In the African tradition, the entire community is held accountable for the child's welfare and upbringing. Hence the proverb "It takes a whole village to raise a child."

The naming ceremony is held separately from a baptism, but both can be held on the same day. In Africa, the naming of a child is of such importance that the parents will spend great resources to make this a festive and memorable event. Naming ceremonies and baby showers should be as individualized as a wedding, and as momentous an occasion.

Each African-American family and community can define the rites, customs, and traditions that are significant to them. And while we should pay particular attention to our African heritage, customs, and celebrations, we are free to include any other customs and traditions to establish our own. For in the final analysis, I believe as African-Americans we must decide what is meaningful to us and to our children, and we must invest these child-related events, celebrations, customs, and traditions with real meaning and feelings so they can be given to and received by successive generations. Please remember, the birth-related rites, events, and celebrations outlined and discussed in this book are just background, planning ideas, and suggestions for your own baby shower or naming ceremony. Though the information contained in this book comes directly from interviews and research done in Africa, some of the rituals have been modified for an American audience. This is your celebration, and the more you personalize your ceremonies, the more meaningful and lasting these customs and traditions will become.

Love is like a baby, it needs to be treated tenderly.

—*Kenyan saying*

The Afrocentric Baby Shower

Motherhood is Supreme.
—*Ashanti proverb*

*I*n African societies, as in American and all other cultures, pregnancy is considered a very serious and special circumstance. However, African culture considers it more spiritual because many African societies believe birth and death are transitions between the earth and the spirit world. Thus many Africans believe a baby is a gift from the spirit world. In America, baby showers are usually associated with fun and games. Afrocentric baby showers offer an added dimension. This chapter will explore and focus on the African-centered, spiritual baby shower.

A BABY SHOWER WITH HERITAGE

In many African countries (because of the high mortality rate), it is forbidden to celebrate the baby before it is born, hence the Tanzanian proverb "Do not make a dress for the baby before the child is born." Often African women will wait until the baby is born to host a baby shower. In some African countries, such as Somalia, women don't

have this taboo and will host a party for the mother and new baby before the birth. This type of baby shower is more serious than the typical American baby shower. An Afrocentric baby shower, called a *Mamatoto* (Kiswahili for "mother and child"), focuses on spiritual oneness of mother and child with their family and with their community. During this ceremony, the guests give the mother many blessings. In South Africa, the Zulus come together with friends and relatives before the birth of a child to decorate the birthing room in beads and artwork. It is believed that the baby will capture and internalize the beauty of the room.

The ceremony begins with the host announcing that the guests should remove their shoes and remain barefoot throughout the ceremony. This also marks the commencement of the celebration. The removal of one's shoes, in African as well as many other countries, is a practice of respect. It also is believed to bring the person closer to the earth, therefore closer to her ancestors.

The host plays an important role in the Afrocentric baby shower. Since every baby shower is different and individualized, the host must plan which events she will utilize and learn the procedures beforehand. The host will act as a guide at the shower by announcing transitions from one activity to the next.

African Dancers, Drummers, Music, and Storytellers

AFRICAN DANCING AND DRUMMING

When traditional dancing is performed in an African village, the villagers surround the dancers by forming a circle. It is customary for the older women to dance first. The older women, some as old as seventy, will cue the younger women when it is their turn to dance by challenging them to a difficult and fast-paced dance step. Your ceremony should also include African dancing. While most libraries have books on African dancing, hiring a dancer for the day to teach the women in attendance an African dance can be a special activity and great fun. It can also provide the guests with an exciting cultural memory.

Drumming has been a part of African history for thousands of years. The power of drumming was so great during slavery that using a drum was outlawed in America. Tap dancing was believed to have developed in place of the drum rhythms.

Djoniba Dance & Drum Centre
37 East 18th Street, 7th fl.
New York, NY 10003
212-477-3464; fax: 212-254-9466
info@djoniba.com

Djoniba's powerful dancers, musicians, dazzling fire eaters, intriguing masks, and breathtaking acrobatic-stilt walkers will transport you to the vibrant world of African music and dance, in a journey that delights the soul and the senses.

Khalidah's North Afrikan Dance Experience
5306 South Cornell Avenue
Chicago, IL 60615
773-324-9305; fax: 773-955-9305
info@khalidahsdance.twoffice.com

The North Afrikan Dance Experience is renowned for its fine adaptations and renditions of dance techniques indigenous to North Africa.

Dimensions Dance Theater
Alice Arts Center
1428 Alice Street, 3rd Floor
Oakland, CA 94612-4004

510-465-3363; fax: 510-465-3364
dimensionsdance@prodigy.net

This dance company offers various programs of African dance and storytelling.

African Caribbean Dance Theatre, Inc.
P.O. Box 10943
Tallahassee, FL 32302
850-539-4087
acdt93@aol.com

The African Caribbean Dance Theatre (ACDT) is a nonprofit youth and adult performing-arts organization. Based in Tallahassee, Florida, ACDT was founded in 1991 by Jevelle and Marcus Robinson to provide an exchange for African and Caribbean dance styles.

AFRICAN MUSIC

Of course, African drums or drum music should be playing in the background at your ceremony. Music along with low lighting and candles (to symbolize torches or firelight) can create the proper ambience to produce a magical nighttime effect. Here are some musical suggestions:

- *Baayo: African Folk Music from Senegal* by Baaba Maal (Mango: An Island Records, Inc.)
- *Africa: Never Stand Still* by various African artists (Ellipsis Arts)
- *African Lullaby* by various artists (Ellipsis Arts)
- *African Voices—Song of Life* by various artists (Emd/Narada)
- *The Best of World Music* by various artists (Putumayo)
- *South African Legends* by various artists (Putumayo)

AFRICAN STORYTELLING

In Africa, the origin of families is passed down from generation to generation through oral tradition. To add a special touch to an Afrocentric baby shower, the hostess may want to hire a storyteller to recount African tales and legends.

When hiring a storyteller ask about:

- the performer's experience
- the appropriate tales to be told
- references to be contacted
- a brochure or literature that he or she has created

- where you can see him or her perform
- what he or she charges
- any special apparatus needed to perform, such as a microphone, stands, a stage, etc.
- how long the show will last
- if you can videotape
- a contract or written agreement that you can use

To locate an African-American storyteller, contact:

Black Storytellers Alliance
Ms. Nothando Zulu, Director
612-529-5864; fax: 612-529-5951
nzulu@blackstorytellers.com

The Alliance helps book performances and assists in scheduling Master Tellers for your organization or cultural event.

AFROCENTRIC PARTY THEMES

Whatever theme you choose for your shower, make sure that it is uplifting and inspiring. You want to welcome the new baby into the world with positive energy from all of the family and friends in attendance. Themes based on other African-American events can be included in the shower theme. Family themes, such as a Kwanzaa-based party or *Umoja Karamu* (an African-American family celebration of unity held on the fourth Sunday of November), work well with baby showers. Here are some ideas to include in your very own Afrocentric baby shower.

KWANZAA SHOWER

Kwanzaa is a family celebration that usually takes place after Christmas and into the New Year. This holiday is an African-American tradition that celebrates the family. The principles and symbolism of Kwanzaa can easily be incorporated into a baby shower. Here are a few examples:

- A great centerpiece for a party table would be a Kwanzaa bush, which is an evergreen bush decorated in the colors of Kwanzaa—red, black, and green. Other centerpieces could include red, black, and green candles in a candelabra or in a *kinara*, a candle-holder that holds the seven candles of Kwanzaa, referred to as *mishumaa saba*. Whatever type of centerpiece you decide on, part of the Kwanzaa tradition includes the centerpiece being displayed on a straw mat called a *mkeka*.

- Fresh fruits and vegetables are symbols of fertility and should always be present at an African-American celebration. During Kwanzaa, these fruits and vegetables are called *mazao*. These fruits and vegetables are then placed on the *mkeka*. Ears of corn, which symbolize offspring, are also placed on the mat. The *kikombe cha umoja*, or communal unity cup, symbolizes unity and is passed around to those in attendance. Homemade gifts called *zawadi* are customary for this type of theme. Baked homemade cookies wrapped in bright cellophane and ribbons make excellent party favors for guests.

- Kwanzaa reinforces the commitment to the family and to the community, and a baby shower is the recognition of the parents' commitment to their newly established family. The parents can recite "A Kwanzaa Promise" to set an example and to teach the seven principles of Kwanzaa to their children every day of the year.

UMOJA KARAMU SHOWER

A Kwanzaa Promise

I promise to uphold the principles of Kwanzaa year-round while living them through the experiences of my new family. Following each of the seven principles—*Umoja* (Unity), *Kujichagulia* (Self-determination), *Ujima* (Collective Work), *Ujamaa* (Cooperative Economics), *Nia* (Purpose), *Kuumba* (Creativity), and *Imani* (Faith)—will assist in allowing my family to grow stronger together through our great African heritage.

Umoja Karamu is a holiday that is celebrated on the last Sunday of November and that symbolizes unity within the family, community, nation, and race. *Umoja Karamu* is celebrated through the presentation of food with narratives of African-American historical periods. This tradition can be instituted into a shower theme by displaying hors d'oeuvres in traditional colors that represent each period. The host can then read narratives from each of those periods to the guests in attendance.

1st Period · The Black family in Africa before slavery. Represented by food that is black; for example, black olives, black beans, and blackberries.

2nd Period · The Black family in slavery. Represented by food that is white; for example, white cheddar cheese, potatoes, and yucca.

3rd Period · The Black family after emancipation. Represented by food that is red; for example, tomatoes, apples, and peppers.

4th Period · The Black family in struggle for liberation. Represented by the color green; for example, celery, lettuce, and grapes.

5th Period · The Black family and hopes for the future. Represented by the color orange or gold; for example, crackers, yam, squash, cheese.

African-American Libation Prayer

Libation prayers thank God and ask the Creator's blessing while inviting African ancestors to join the celebration for good luck. The ancestors are acknowledged by asking them to come, starting from the East (the direction of Africa), then following with the West, the North, and finishing with the South. A sample prayer is as follows:

"We ask God's blessing here today as we offer this sacrifice of thanks to our Creator. I pour this libation to ask that our African ancestors join us from the East [while pouring the liquid on the ground in the direction of the East, then continuing accordingly as you recite], from the West, from the North, and from the South. With God in the forefront, our ancestors standing strong behind us, and our families beside us, there is nothing we cannot accomplish. Amen."

THE LIBATION

As in many African ceremonies, the Afrocentric baby shower should begin with a libation. A libation is a ritual act that was once outlawed by Christians and Muslims, who associated them with pagan or non-Semitic deities. Libations consist of the pouring of a drink as a sacrifice, offering, or prayer. The traditional method for libation is quite basic and simple, which is part of its beauty and significance in African societies.

To perform a ritual libation, place a liquid in any type of vessel or goblet, preferably one that has or can be assigned some lasting spiritual significance. It may be simple or exotic. Then the liquid is poured onto the earth, onto some event-meaningful object, or into another vessel or bowl. While pouring, recite a prayer.

In the Yoruban tradition, libations are poured to various gods. The Yoruba pour libations onto fires, stones, statues of the gods, individuals, or simply onto the ground, depending on the purpose. By making a libation, African women reaffirm their spiritual nature and place in the cosmos.

For Africans and many other peoples, wine traditionally represents the blood of the earth. Wine is considered a suitable offering for virtually any purpose. White wines as well as red wines share the same symbolism. Even beer has meaning. To Africans, a libation of beer represents an oath to your family and community. Beer libations can be performed to strengthen friendship, when giving or receiving an oath, and to cement an agreement or to form a compact.

A libation of milk can be extremely meaningful. To Africans, milk represents family, kindness, and acceptance. Milk libations are given as thanks for anything associated with the family or relatives, such as in a libation of thanks for the pregnancy of a woman in the family. Milk can be used as a peace offering as well. Libations of milk are also poured when someone is seeking forgiveness, as an act of humility, or as acknowledgment of one's own shortcomings.

Cider or strawberry wine is appropriate for libations associated with matters of community, fun, or enjoyment. Thus, a cider or strawberry wine libation may be offered for the success of the pregnancy or for the baby shower.

Hard liquor and spirits, such as whiskey, vodka, gin, or rice wine, are associated with libations poured for strong reasons. For example, a person might use a libation of spirits in supplication for the things he wants most in the world, to fulfill his personal destiny, or for the purposes of casting or avoiding curses. Thus, if the birth of a healthy child is one of the mother's greatest desires, she may wish to make a libation with spirits. Always remember that the mother-of-honor should not consume alcohol when she is pregnant. Nor should she consume alcohol if she has recently given birth or is nursing. Guests may want to refrain from drinking alcoholic beverages out of respect for the mother-of-honor.

These libations can be poured from any vessel, whether a cup, a bowl, or a dish. However, Africans often use ceremonial or special vessels that they have carved or made specifically for libations. Many of them have the shape of an animal.

A libation can be poured for any specific purpose or for general purposes. As a ritual act, the libation is a demonstration of our deep respect, concern, and desire for the fulfillment of our wishes and prayers. As an overt act, libations also illustrate our faith in deeds. Thus, a libation is a prayer of deeds as much as a prayer of words.

Many contemporary African baby showers begin with a libation of water poured from a wooden cup into a plant and a prayer offering in honor of our ancestors. It is asked aloud that your ancestors or the living-dead be with you as official guests of the occasion and for them to add their blessing from every direction (meaning from North, South, East, and West) to all ritual libations.

The Community Journal

A very memorable activity consists of creating the community journal. Distribute sheets of notebook paper that can later be fastened in a binder. Each guest should write a letter to the baby or to the mother-of-honor, bestowing wishes or giving their best advice and tips for adjusting to the new world and for motherhood. Special items, such as pressed flowers, artwork, and photos, can be added to the community journal. This makes an intimate keepsake for the mother-of-honor, or the entries can be transferred to the baby's keepsake journal.

THE TRUST WALK

Another activity based on traditional African rituals is the trust walk. The trust walk is enacted to symbolize the support of all the women present for the new mother. To begin the trust walk, blindfold the mother-of-honor and form two lines. As the mother walks between the two lines, each of the guests should gently touch her shoulder and forehead. They should then take turns rubbing her back and hugging her. This gesture of kindness and solidarity is designed to remind the new mother that she may not now see where she is going, but she is going to get there, even though she may not know or see who will help her along the way. She will come to realize that those whom she can see and those whom she can't see will always be there for her.

THE SISTER-CIRCLE

After the trust walk, the furniture in the room should be set in a circle around an Afrocentric chair or stool. In African societies, the circle is symbolic and serves as a protective ring around the mother to keep evil and harm from her and the unborn infant. The mother-of-honor should be in the middle of the sister-circle under a Kente cloth umbrella decorated especially for the baby shower.

Starting with the elders in attendance, all the mothers in the sister-circle should take turns sharing their experiences of childbirth with the new mother while holding her hand. Keeping the circle intact, the guests should stand and circle around the mother-of-honor; then each guest takes a turn at giving the new mom words of wisdom or advice. This should be done while attaching gifts of money, instead of bows, to her headdress, as Ghanaian women do. This ritual is believed to protect and help the family in raising the new baby.

When this part of the celebration is finished, the mother-of-honor meditates while sitting in the sister-circle, allowing each guest's positive energy to flow to her. Each guest should bring to the circle a poem or song to share.

THE COMMUNITY QUILT

The African-American quilting tradition is old, strong, and ongoing. Quilts and blankets have been used for many years to celebrate births, weddings, and graduations. They have also served as a historical album that tells the story of the relationships of certain groups and families. You can easily involve your guests in an activity designed to produce an heirloom quilt, which can serve either as a functional blanket for the baby or as a wall hanging to commemorate the occasion.

To make an heirloom quilt at your Afrocentric baby shower, begin a few days before the event. Purchase or prepare two different types of fabric squares that complement each other. These should be approximately four square inches in size. Be sure to purchase or cut out enough for all of your guests. Provide your shower guests with the proper equipment and different types of embellishments, such as various fabric textures, fabric glue, scissors, fabric paint, and pens, which the guests can use to design and personalize their own square or squares.

If you decide to use decorations or embellishments, like cowry shells, buttons, or anything that may come off, then the quilt should be used only as a wall hanging, because the small pieces could be a choking hazard for the new baby.

Textured fabrics, such as felt, corduroy, velvet, silk, cotton, tapestry, and natural fibers, make excellent materials for a functional baby quilt.

Have each of the guests design her own personal square for the baby. If none of the guests has the time or expertise, the hostess of the event may want to hire a quilter to put the pieces together during or after the event. Another method is to mail the fabric square in a padded envelope with the shower invitation, along with an explanation and directions for the guest to make her square ahead of time. This way, the guests can include the sentimental fabric pieces or memorabilia that they may have at home. At the event, the guests can tell the story of their contributions to the quilt. Provide extra quilt squares and embellishments

Shower Etiquette Tips

- Don't make a big deal if a guest arrives early. If the guest arrives too early, invite the guest to the area where you are working to watch or help.
- Don't make a big deal if a guest arrives late. Start the party as planned. The late guest can catch up when she arrives.
- Remember to take plenty of photographs. It is a good idea to scatter several disposable cameras around the room so that your guests can take their own personal photos of the shower. This also helps capture the spontaneity of the celebration for posterity. There are companies that will emboss the date of the shower on decorative disposable cameras, and developing is included in the price (see the resource guide).

for guests who may have forgotten to prepare a square in advance. The community quilt can become a valuable family heirloom, and it is a fine way for your guests to add a personal part of themselves to the baby's life.

THE RITUAL CLOSING

Toward the end of the ceremony, ask all of the guests to sit in the sister-circle once again. Taking turns, this is the time for each guest to go to the expectant mother and whisper a blessing while touching the new mother on the shoulder or the stomach. There is an adage in Nigeria about the importance of giving inspiration through touch. It states: "Can the drum talk without being touched?"

two

Religious Elements

Good things need a lot of
prayers to keep them intact.
—*Yoruban proverb*

*A*frican-Americans traditionally have included religion in all major life-changing events. So, whether you choose to have an Afrocentric or African-American baby shower, you may want to include a religious component as part of your event.

PRAYERS AND BLESSINGS

Some hostesses may want to introduce religious elements, such as blessings, songs, and prayers. This is the time to remember God and our African ancestors,

and all they've done for us and will do for the community, the new mother, and the infant she will soon bring into God's world.

Reverence and worship are meaningful to African and African-American women alike. Some women will naturally prefer or request only Christian songs and prayers. But today many more African-Americans want to honor, worship, and revere their African

15

ancestors. It is vitally important to remember that the religious beliefs of others should be treated as respectfully and as reverently as we treat our own.

Most African women believe God is transcendental, and like the Christian God, the Creator sometimes seems remote. But they also know that God is immanent and manifested in nature, in both objects and phenomena. Thus, African women can find and worship God in any place and at any time.

Similarly, Africans use blessings for almost anything, from greeting a friend or neighbor to rituals and celebrations. So blessings may be used when welcoming guests as well as when closing the Afrocentric or African-American baby shower. Blessings are similar from one African country to the next. These blessings were believed to come true for an individual, if said by enough people. Here are some typical African blessings:

May God walk with you this day! [Blessing of support]
May God preserve you and keep you until you see your children's children!
[Blessing for a long life]
May God bless you with fruit! [Blessing for children and wealth]
May God make your feet light! [Blessing for prosperity]
May God give you a clean face! [Blessing for virtuousness]
May God make your forehead big! [Blessing for beauty]

Some appropriate African prayers include the following, which is offered by Masai women to bring rain. Because rain is essential to all life, the prayer is used for the general well-being of the community, livestock or wildlife, and nature in its entirety.

The hostess or mother-of-honor can serve as the female leader. First, she says one part, then the guests can sing or recite the response traditionally given by those present for the ceremony:

Leader: We need herbs on the earth's back!
Others: Hie! Wae! Almighty God.
Leader: The father of Nasira has conquered, has conquered.
Others: The highlands and also the lowlands of our vast country, which belongs to thee,
O God.
Leader: May this be our year, ours in plenty.
Others: O messenger of Mbatian's son.

Another prayer typically offered by Ashanti women each morning can be said at any time:

Morning has risen.
God, take away from us every pain, every ill, every mishap.
God, let us come [or go] safely home.

Another African prayer involving mother and child comes from the Aro of Sierra Leone. While the prayer is traditionally offered for a sick child, it can be altered or offered as is for the well-being of an unborn child. The mother begins the prayer by singing, chanting, or intoning the first verse. The women serve as the chorus and respond after each verse the mother prays:

The Mother: O spirits of the past, this little one I hold is my child. She is your child also; therefore, be gracious unto her.

The Women: She has come into a world of trouble: sickness is in the world, and cold, and pain; the pain you knew and the sickness with which you were familiar.

The Mother: Let her sleep in peace, for there is healing in sleep. Let none among you be angry with me or with my child.

The Women: Let her grow, let her become strong. Let her become full grown. Then will she offer such a sacrifice to you that will delight your heart.

Among the Nuer, prayer is considered an activity to be performed at any time, day or night. Because they are happy when they talk to God, they often pray as they go about their daily routines. Here is a prayer the Nuer use regularly and for general well-being:

Our Father, it is Thy universe, it is Thy will.
Let us be at peace, let the souls of Thy people be cool.
Thou art our Father, remove all evil from our path.

Opening of Gifts

In closing, ask the guests to be seated with their gifts. It's usually best to have the mother-of-honor open gifts toward the end of the ceremony. At this time, a prayer of thanks to God and for the guests could be led by the mom-to-be.

The hostess can either do it herself or ask someone else to sit next to the mother-of-honor as she opens gifts. This person should record the gifts and the name of the person who gave each item. This list will be used for writing thank-you notes after the shower. After each gift is opened, be sure to pass it around the room so all the guests can see it. Remember to save all the gift cards for the baby's scrapbook.

After the food or the meal is served, a nice prayer that can be used comes from the Barotse:

I thank Thee for the meat, which Thou givest me.
Today Thou hast stood by me.

Many other African prayers can be found in library books on African religion; also, search the Web. Of course, the hostess, guests, and mother-of-honor can create and offer their own African, Christian, Muslim, or other prayers and blessings.

CLOSING BENEDICTION

Usually an African-American ceremony of great importance will close with a benediction. The benediction is a good time for another libation, poured for the health and welfare of mother and child, or for the community at large. In bidding one another farewell, the Mende say, "May God walk you well!" The Shilluk say, "May God guard you!"

Here is an example of a closing benediction that provides strength in unity:

We end this ceremony as descendants of the great African men and women who refused to die during their voyage across the Middle Passage between Africa and the New World. Though they were enslaved and oppressed, we—their legacy—are still here. For them we pour and say this libation. [The libation is poured on the ground toward the East, West, North, and then South.] It is our responsibility to continue to protect the rights our ancestors fought for, and for this we ask them to lend us their strength. For the unborn baby and his or her family we say this libation, so they as a unit will

Thank-You Notes

Everyone likes to be appreciated, so remember to send out thank-you notes. A brief handwritten thank-you identifying the gift and adding a kind word or perhaps an African proverb will be especially appreciated. Thank-you notes should be mailed out by the mother-of-honor within one week of the shower.

At some baby showers, the hostess passes around envelopes at the party for everyone to self-address. This is a good idea because it makes it easy for the expectant or new mother, who then doesn't have to address any thank-you cards.

Birth Announcements

After the baby is born, the new mother should also send birth announcements to all of the shower guests. Don't forget to use postage stamps with images of African-Americans to mail all of your cards!

care for this child so that this child achieves the greatness of those who came before. To this, we all say, "Harambee." [Everyone lifts their right hand to the sky and repeats "Harambee," a Kiswahili word that means "unity," while making a fist in the air and pulling their hand down.]

Shower Etiquette Tips

- Don't start cleaning up before the guests leave. This is only acceptable if you have a guest who has overstayed her welcome.
- Don't ask the guests to stay and help you clean up. Wait until after the party to clean. If you are too tired, wait until the next morning, or hire a service.
- If you forgot to send out the thank-you cards for the shower that you had three months ago, don't assume it is too late to send them now! Send the thank-you cards anyway. Most guests will assume that your pregnancy prevented you from doing it in a timely fashion. Just make sure to send out the shower thank-you cards before the birth announcements!
- Remember to take lots of photographs!

Food for Thought

In Africa, as in African-American culture, it is considered extremely rude not to offer your visiting guests something to eat, even if there isn't enough food for the host's own family. If you are a guest from another country visiting an African family for dinner, they may give you an infinite invitation to return and stay with them as an unofficial member of their family. Celebrations for the birth of a child can be majestic in Africa. Even the poorest of all families will save all of their resources just for this grand event. The meal is part of the main focus. It is carefully prepared by the womenfolk. In Senegal, many of the kitchens are located outside on cement rooftops. There the women gather socially to prepare the grand meal.

AFRICAN-AMERICAN DISHES FOR ENTERTAINING

American baby showers are traditionally scheduled between meals; therefore, a large

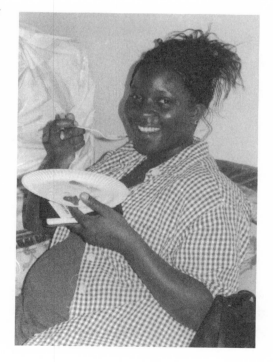

menu isn't necessary. Serve light foods, just to hold your guests over until their next meal, and save the preparation of a grand feast for the baby's naming ceremony, after the baby is born.

On the following pages are various soul food recipes, which have traditionally been enjoyed by African-American families celebrating the birth of a new baby. These recipes are just suggestions. As you plan your event, you may want to add your own family's recipes and traditions.

THE CAKE

Though cake isn't part of most African celebrations, cake is usually the centerpiece of any African-American baby shower. If you choose to have a cake, you can use your creativity to bake your own Afrocentric cake or purchase one from a bakery. Commercial cakes can be made to order with your own African design. There are also bakeries that make specialized Afrocentric cakes (see the resource guide at the back of the book).

Of course, you can always bake your own cake and frost it in blue-and-pink frosting. One of the easiest baby shower cakes to make is a Swahili Baby-Block Cake, which is simply three square carrot cakes with a Swahili parental greeting on each of them.

Swahili Baby-Block Cake

3 boxes carrot cake mix
3 cans white frosting
Red and blue food coloring
Cake letters or tube icing

Bake the cake according to the package directions, using three 9 x 9 x 2–inch square baking pans. Using two separate mixing bowls, blend one can of frosting with a small amount of red food coloring to make the pink icing; use another bowl to mix a can of frosting with blue food coloring to make a baby blue icing. After frosting, decorate the cake baby blocks with the letters *A*, *B*, and *C*. Draw each letter in a different color of icing (alternate pink and blue).

Under the letter *A*, write the Swahili word *Abee*, which means "I am on the way." For the letter *B*, write the word *Barikwa* in pink icing, which means "Your blessing," and beneath the letter *C*, write the word *Chunga* in blue icing, which means "Look after me." The Swahili words on your block cake will then translate into the phrase "I am on the way, your blessing, so look after me."

SERVES 20

Another easy baby shower cake idea calls for a Bundt cake and a baby bottle. Buy or bake the Bundt cake and decorate it with icing and pink-and-blue candy sprinkles. Then fill the baby bottle with colorful candy and tie a ribbon around the bottle's neck. Stick the baby bottle, filled with candy and tied with ribbon, in the middle of the cake.

BEVERAGES

Some ideas for tasty party beverages include Sherbet Punch, Baby-Bath Punch, lemonade, and regular and decaffeinated coffees and teas. To keep punch and lemonade from getting diluted during the party, freeze some of the juice in ice cube trays or a large container to make "ice" for the punch.

Decorate Your Cake with Words

African Proverbs

"Motherhood is supreme."—Ivory Coast
"God could not be everywhere so he sent Mother."—Egypt
"The source of human love is the mother."—Zaire
"A mother is gold."—Nigeria
"Children are the reward of life."—Zaire

Other Baby Shower–Cake Sayings

Showers of Happiness
Pink or Blue, We Welcome You
Diapers & Pins—Now the Fun Begins
Diapers & Pins—A New Life Begins
Welcome Precious Baby
Welcome Baby_____ [Fill in baby's name, if known, or use surname]
Happy Labor Day!
Here's a Whole New Meaning to Life!

Quotes About Motherhood

The sweetest sounds to mortals given
Are heard in Mother, Home and Heaven.
                    —W. G. Brown

What is home without a mother?
                    —Alice Hawthorne

Her children arise and call her blessed.
          —Old Testament, Proverbs 31:28

For the hand that rocks the cradle is the hand that rules the world.
                                        —W. S. Ross

Mother is the name for God in the lips and hearts of little children.
                                        —W. M. Thackeray

Entertaining African-American Style!

Be sure to check out all the great ideas for entertaining found in the *African-American Kitchen* by Angela Shelf Medearis. This book has an entire section devoted to planning a menu for an Afrocentric baby shower. Culinary delights, such as a frosted brown-sugar spice cake, can really set the tone for the menu. The book is chock-full of delightful dishes and hors d'oeuvres with an African-American flavor. Put a little soul in your food!

Other African-American cookbooks that work well with baby showers are *Traditional South African Cookery* by Hildagonda Duckitt; *A Taste of Heritage* by Chef Joe Randall and Toni Tipton-Martin; and *The Healthy Soul Food Cookbook* by Wilbert Jones.

Sherbet Punch

Thaw 1 gallon of pastel-colored sherbet and place in a punch bowl. Add 1 liter of 7Up. Mix lightly.

SERVES 15

Baby-Bath Punch

A cute idea for a punch bowl is to use a yellow plastic baby tub. Remove the foam inserts. Fill it up with blue Kool-Aid, and float a couple of rubber duckies or plastic flowers in it. (wash them thoroughly beforehand, of course).

SERVES APPROXIMATELY 20 PEOPLE

FINGER FOOD AND HORS D'OEUVRES

The hostess should find out what the favorite African-American dishes of the mother-of-honor and the guests are. An African-American hors d'oeuvres menu for a baby shower may include such appetizing delights as Kickin' Chicken Wingettes, Lil' Angel Eggs (instead of "deviled" eggs), Baby Beef Barbecue Ribs, and Lil' Sweet Pea Salad.

Another significant dish is the fruit salad. In Africa, fruit symbolizes new life. If possible, for a real treat, order from your local or specialty grocer some unique African fruits, such as monkey bread, from the baobab tree; plantains; or other available fruits, such as mangoes, bananas, coconuts, and melons.

Soul Food

Though this traditional African-American fare has long been popular in the old Southern states, the term itself is actually relatively new. It became part of the modern usage in approximately 1960. The expression *soul food* is thought to have derived from the cultural spirit and soul-satisfying flavors of African-American food.

—from *The Food Lover's Companion* by Sharon Tyler Herbst

If you would like to try your hand at an African dish, it's best to start with something simple, such as Hot Plantain Crisps or Moroccan Spiced Olives. Plantains are a fruit, similar to the banana, that is indigenous to Africa and has been eaten as a delicacy for centuries. Olives are a staple crop in Morocco and are served in many types of African dishes.

Other foods that work great at showers include cold cut–and–cheese trays and other dishes that can be easily prepared and served. It is best to serve at least eight hors d'oeuvres per person. Try to keep the dishes simple.

If you are planning to have an outdoor baby shower, there are several other possibilities. Of course, you can plan on having a barbecue, an all-time African-American favorite. But you might want to consider a fish fry or a crab feast. Serving light foods at a baby shower also makes it reasonable to use paper goods. This will eliminate time-consuming and unwanted clean-up chores.

It is also possible to keep the African-centered theme going by using Kente paper plates, cups, and napkins. These and other decorative items are available from the American Greetings Company (see the resource guide).

Make sure your foods for the shower are kept simple and easy. Here is a sample of a basic Afrocentric baby shower menu that should give you a few ideas for your own celebration.

Afrocentric Baby Shower Menu

Hot Hors d'Oeuvres

Kickin' Chicken Wingettes
Baby Beef Barbecue Ribs
Hot Plantain Chips

Cold Hors d'Oeuvres

Lil' Angel Eggs
Lil' Sweet Pea Salad
Baby Carriage Fruit Basket
Moroccan Spiced Olives

Beverages

Sherbet Punch
Baby-Bath Punch

Dessert

Swahili Baby Block Cake

AFRICAN-AMERICAN BABY SHOWER RECIPES

Kickin' Chicken Wingettes

1 bag (2 lbs.) chicken wingettes

Salt substitute and pepper

½ cup catsup

¼ cup spicy brown mustard

¼ cup hot sauce

¼ cup finely chopped onion

1 tablespoon honey

1 tablespoon vinegar

1 clove garlic, minced

Preheat oven to 375 degrees. Rinse the chicken wingettes well and pat them dry. Season the wings with a salt substitute and pepper. Place the pieces in a single layer on a baking sheet. Bake for 20 minutes. Drain the fat from the baking sheet.

Combine the remaining ingredients in a bowl to make the sauce. Brush the chicken with the sauce and bake for 10 minutes. Turn the wings over and brush again with the sauce. Bake for 5 to 10 minutes or until chicken is tender.

Cook chicken well to avoid illness from salmonella bacteria. Don't forget to provide lots of napkins!

SERVES 10

Baby Beef Barbecue Ribs

6 pounds baby back beef ribs

1 teaspoon meat tenderizer

1 teaspoon seasoning, such as
   Mrs. Dash, or seasoning salt

2 cups chopped onions

2 garlic cloves, minced

2 tablespoons cooking oil

2 eight-ounce cans tomato sauce

½ cup spicy brown mustard

½ cup honey

½ cup brown sugar

6 tablespoons lemon juice

4 tablespoons Worcestershire sauce

2 tablespoons prepared mustard

1 teaspoon celery seed

Preheat oven to 350 degrees. Boil the ribs in a large pot of water for one hour. Remove the ribs and pat them dry. Season ribs with meat tenderizer and seasoning. Then place ribs, bone side down, on a rack in a shallow roasting pan. Bake in oven at 350 degrees for 1 hour. Pour off the fat regularly.

While the ribs are cooking, prepare the barbecue sauce. In a medium saucepan, cook the onion and garlic in hot oil until tender. Stir in the remaining ingredients. Simmer for 15 minutes, stirring occasionally.

Brush the sauce over the ribs, then cover and bake the ribs for 30 minutes or until they are well done. Occasionally spoon the sauce over the ribs. Serve the remaining sauce for dipping with the ribs.

SERVES 10

Lil' Angel Eggs

6 eggs, hard-cooked

¼ cup low-fat mayonnaise
    or salad dressing

1 teaspoon yellow mustard

Paprika

To cook the eggs, gently lower room-temperature eggs into a large saucepan of simmering water. The saucepan should be large enough to fit the eggs in a single layer; there should be enough simmering water to cover the eggs. Simmer for 12 to 15 minutes on low heat, to avoid cracking. Cool the eggs by plunging them into cold running water. When cooled, peel the eggs, then halve lengthwise and remove the yolks. Place the yolks in a bowl and mash them with a fork. Add the mayonnaise and mustard and blend well.

Use two spoons to fill the egg white cavities with the yolk mixture, or use a cake-decorating bag with a large star tip to make a fancier egg. Sprinkle paprika over the eggs for color.

SERVES 12

Lil' Sweet Pea Salad

1 pound spiral macaroni

10 cups sweet peas
  (optional: fresh, canned, or frozen)

4 teaspoons finely chopped basil

2 garlic cloves, finely minced

4 teaspoons sugar

½ teaspoon chili paste

½ teaspoon paprika

½ teaspoon black pepper

2 teaspoons dry mustard

1 cup apple cider vinegar

1 cup light salad oil

Lettuce for serving platter

Cook the macaroni according to package directions, then cool to room temperature. Cook the peas, if not canned. Place the macaroni and prepared peas in a large serving bowl. In a separate mixing bowl, combine basil, garlic, sugar, chili paste, paprika, black pepper, and mustard. Whisk in the vinegar and salad oil.

Pour the mixture over the macaroni and peas, and mix thoroughly. Chill at least 1 hour before serving. Serve on a bed of lettuce.

SERVES 12

*The watermelon fruit salad is an all-time favorite
for baby showers. Shown here is another version of
the many types of fruit baskets you can create.*

Baby Carriage Fruit Basket

1 oblong watermelon

10 strawberries, halved lengthwise

6 kiwi fruits, cut into chunks

4 bananas, sliced thin

4 apples, sliced, cored, and seeded,
  cut into chunks

4 oranges, peeled and separated

2 mangoes, cut into chunks

2 cans pineapple chunks

1 cantaloupe, scooped into balls

1 melon, scooped into balls

Seedless grapes, white or red

Dark sweet cherries, halved and pitted

Lemon juice

Leaf lettuce

1 cup real fruit punch

2 pipe cleaners

Cut a thin, flat slice off the watermelon lengthwise; this will prevent it from rolling. Slice the watermelon halfway through in the center, width-wise. Be sure to stop halfway. Then, standing the melon on its end, cut the watermelon lengthwise and stop at the first cut. Remove the quarter section of the watermelon. The watermelon shell should now resemble a hooded baby carriage.

Using an ice cream scoop or a deep spoon, scoop out the entire watermelon shell. Save the watermelon balls to add to the fruit salad.

With the peel still on the orange, cut four sliced circles for wheels, which will be used later, then peel or cut up the remaining orange. Mix all the cut fruit in a large bowl. Spray the fruit with lemon juice to prevent it from browning. Then mix well again. Pour on the fruit punch and mix thoroughly.

Line the watermelon shell with leafy lettuce, then add the fruit. Chill for at least 2 hours. Bend the pipe cleaners into the shape of a baby carriage handle, and use the toothpicks to fasten the orange slice "wheels" to the sides of the baby carriage. The Baby Carriage Fruit Basket makes a colorful and decorative centerpiece. Display it on the table.

SERVES 15

Baby Shower Salad Bar

For a wholesome and healthy menu, and a quick and inexpensive meal, try a self-serve salad bar. This is always a big hit with the ladies, and it cuts down on the amount of serving for the hostess.

Simply prepare serving bowls full of lettuce, spinach, tomatoes, mushrooms, broccoli, cauliflower, cucumbers, onions, shredded carrots, radishes, shredded cheese, sliced boiled eggs, meat cubes, olives, and croutons. Place forks and bowls on the table, and serve with a variety of low-fat salad dressings.

An African calabash

The African Calabash Bowl

For that cultural touch, serve your hors d'oeuvres and foods in Afrocentric baskets, dishes, and bowls, such as a calabash bowl.

A calabash is a large, decorated bowl that is used for everything, from carrying milk to bathing newborn babies. It is made from one of the larger types of gourd. These bowls are usually painted in beautiful and traditional designs. These exotic bowls have frequently been used to serve foreign and African dignitaries and royalty. Calabashes sometimes feature decorations and designs that have a particular tribal significance or symbols that denote the status of a woman. Some calabashes are passed down from one generation to the next and are cared for by women. They are exhibited in elaborate displays only for special occasions, such as during a naming ceremony. For instance, young Cameroon women design these gourds and calabash bowls to indicate their new status as a mother. Serving food in a beautiful calabash is a fine African tradition and one worthy of being honored in African-American communities and incorporated into baby showers.

Special African Healing Dishes

In some countries in Africa, the new mother is served a porridge, similar to oatmeal, that is mixed with sour cream and nutmeg. This dish helps heal her womb. Not only is the dish served to the mother, it is also served to each of the guests, along with a kola nut.

Porridge

Hot Plantain Crisps

4 plantains
4 teaspoons lemon juice
4 teaspoons ground ginger

4 teaspoons cayenne pepper
Oil for frying

Slice the plantains lengthwise from end to end, then peel. Cut into rounds approximately a half-inch thick. Sprinkle lemon juice over the pieces. Cover for fifteen minutes to moisten. In a separate bowl, mix the ginger and cayenne pepper.

Heat one-quarter inch of oil in a heavy skillet until a test piece of plantain sputters. Place the plantain pieces a few at a time in the spice mixture to coat surfaces, then transfer them to the skillet. Fry until the outsides are golden crisp. With a slotted spoon, remove plantains and lay them on an absorbent paper towel to cool. Serve hot.

SERVES 10

Moroccan Spiced Olives

1 tablespoon olive oil
1 teaspoon cumin seeds
1 teaspoon fennel seeds
1 teaspoon coriander seeds
¼ teaspoon ground cardamom
1 pinch crushed red pepper flakes

1 pinch ground nutmeg
1 pinch cinnamon
1½ cups green olives, room temperature
1 tablespoon lemon juice
1 tablespoon orange juice
3 garlic cloves, minced

Gently heat olive oil and spices (cumin, fennel, and coriander seeds, cardamom, crushed red pepper flakes, nutmeg, and cinnamon) in a small skillet over low heat, approximately 2 minutes, just until the seeds begin to pop. Remove from heat and add the olives. Mix until completely coated. Stir in the remaining ingredients. Refrigerate in an airtight plastic container for at least 4 hours. Drain and serve at room temperature.

SERVES 12

Shower Etiquette Tips

• Don't serve alcohol at a baby shower. It's not healthy for the mother-of-honor, and by not serving alcohol, you are showing your respect.
• Don't stay in the kitchen preparing and serving foods. Enjoy the party and stay with your guests.
• Don't wash dishes during the party. Wait until after the party when all the guests have left.
• Don't let your guests wash the dishes! Just jokingly say, "We never wash dishes here, we just throw them out."

The Cravings of Pregnant African Women!

Some of the foods East Africans favored and that are craved by pregnant women include unsweetened plantains, white potatoes, milk, eggs, fish, and clay! Yes, I said clay! Some of the foods that are believed to be taboo and are strictly avoided by African women include salt, ribbed meat, sugar cane, onions, sweet plantain, and white ants! By implication, does that mean black ants and red ants are okay? Yummy!

—Kilbride and Kilbride, 1990

four

Planning the Baby Shower

Time passes quickly, so use it well.
—*Nigerian proverb*

The African-American baby shower differs from the African event only in the type of activities and rituals employed. Unlike the Afrocentric shower, this type of baby shower includes many American influences. Though this shower is more Americanized, the decor can still be Afrocentric, and the party favors, prizes, and gifts can also have a distinct African flair.

WHERE AND WHEN TO HOST AN AFRICAN-AMERICAN BABY SHOWER

The best time to host an African-American baby shower, of course, is when a woman is pregnant and will soon deliver a beautiful, bubbling brown baby. Traditionally, in America, a baby shower is given four to six weeks before the baby is due. Unless the woman has had an ultrasound and the parents have requested this information, this timing doesn't give the guests

An African Taboo

In some cultures in Africa, to admit publicly that one is pregnant before you are obviously showing is taboo. It is believed that a woman's pregnancy may arouse jealousy in another and someone may bewitch or curse the baby.

—Afua, a woman from Togo, West Africa

the advantage of knowing the baby's gender. Consequently, it is difficult for them to select masculine or feminine colors and to purchase appropriate clothes. Today, more and more baby showers are given after the child is born. This not only makes gift giving easier, but in fact it is also more in line with traditional African beliefs and celebrations. Indeed, in many African and European countries, it is considered bad luck to celebrate the baby before it is born.

According to Dr. Abu Abarry, a professor in the African-American Studies Department at Temple University, "the unborn child belongs to the spiritual world before it is born. Once the baby is born and it has survived, sometime within the first seven days, is time for the celebration." This seven-day period also allows time for the mother to recuperate.

If the parents aren't planning to hold a naming ceremony, it may be best to wait at least four weeks after the baby is born in order to give the new mom and baby time to bond and synchronize their internal clocks, or biorhythms. This also gives the shower sponsor time to plan ahead. To get things done, plan over an extended period of time, instead of in a one-week rush. If you are the sponsor and are going to hold the shower before the baby is born, don't choose a day too close to the mother's due date.

The rule of thumb for setting the shower date is: Earlier, is better, but not before the sixth month. This way, parents can get the things they need even if the mother is on bed rest, or they can get someone else to shop for them.

Whenever you decide to hold the shower, before or after the baby's birth, remember to be considerate of your guests' work schedules. If the shower is on a weekday, it should be held in the evening. If the shower is held on a weekend, plan to have it in the afternoon or evening to let people run errands and attend religious services. For coworkers who are planning a shower, your boss would most likely appreciate having the shower at lunchtime or after work.

Somalia Sisterhood

Expectant mothers benefit from a strong network of women within the Somali culture. Unlike the practices of many other countries in Africa, Somali women hold a celebration for the pregnant mother before the birth of a child, as a gesture of support.

Whatever date you select, always remember that babies have their own schedules, so be prepared to reschedule if necessary.

Plan to start the shower approximately twenty to thirty minutes after the scheduled time so that everyone has a chance to get there, introduce themselves, and mingle before the shower activities actually begin.

The shower should last no longer than four hours. This is enough time to eat, play games, open gifts, have cake, and socialize. Be sure to include an ending time on the invitation, so that you won't have any guests showing up late.

Like Americans, African women come together at the mother-of-honor's home to celebrate the baby's birth. But a baby shower can be held almost anywhere. The most popular places are in the home or at work. Sometimes homes and offices have space limitations. Some of the nontraditional sites listed here may give a larger group more room and provide easy clean-up for the host. Interesting places to have a baby shower include:

TRADITIONAL

in the mother's home
at a relative's home
at a friend's home
in the workplace

CONTEMPORARY

a backyard
at a park
at a hotel
at the hospital after delivery
in a restaurant
at a pool
in a church hall
on a boat
at a golf course
at an amusement park
in a bowling alley
at an African-American museum

at an African art gallery
on the beach
on a baseball field
in public gardens and arboretums

Usually a family member, close friends, or co-workers will host a shower for the pregnant woman. Sometimes the expectant mother may have several baby showers, planned by both family and co-workers. Therefore, it is necessary to collaborate with others so that conflicts and duplications don't arise, such as two baby showers on the same day. If you are a co-worker or a friend, consult with the family and vice versa.

The Village Marketplace

The Fulani ethnic group of Sudan holds many social celebrations right in the marketplace. The atmosphere is festive. The excitement of a child's birth is contagious. Celebrating it in the marketplace, where there are many people gathered from various regions, also spreads the news of a baby's birth for several miles and even to other communities.

African marketplace, Dakar, Senegal

Not My Shower

A girl I worked with was going to throw a baby shower for me. The more she discussed it with me, the more obvious it became that she was inviting her friends instead of mine. Well, I made up an excuse and got out of it. A shower is personal. It is for you and your close friends to celebrate the new baby. Don't let anyone ruin it for you.

—Tamika, Philadelphia, Pennsylvania

 **TIMELINE**

THREE MONTHS PRIOR TO THE EVENT

- Decide on a theme for your Afrocentric baby shower. You can have a . . .

  regal theme

  Kente or mudcloth theme

  theme that focuses on one country in Africa, such as Egypt or Kenya.

- Decide if the shower will be a surprise.
- Determine the location.
- Set a budget.
- Plan a guest list.
- Check with the mother-of-honor about making a gift list or registry.
- Order, purchase, or begin making your invitations.
- Start looking for appropriate props and decorations.
- Call to arrange for the drummers, dancers, and/or storytellers.

TWO MONTHS PRIOR TO THE EVENT

- Begin making party favors.
- Confirm the site for the shower.
- Plan food or hire a caterer.

ONE MONTH PRIOR TO THE EVENT

- Mail the invitations with a map and a self-addressed, stamped envelope to make the RSVP convenient. Each postcard should have two boxes to check:

  ☐ I will be able to attend.
  ☐ I won't be able to attend.

- Confirm the arrangements for drummers, dancers, and storytellers.

ONE WEEK BEFORE THE EVENT

- Call guests who have not RSVP'd.
- Purchase groceries and supplies.

ONE DAY PRIOR TO THE EVENT

- Clean.
- Set up the room with chairs.
- Begin cooking.

THE BIG DAY ARRIVES . . .

- Decorate the room.
- Prepare the food.
- Get dressed.

The Long-Distance Baby Shower

When I had my son, I was 3,000 miles from home. A group of good friends decided that distance wouldn't stop them from throwing a baby shower for me. One day, the mailman delivered a huge box. Inside were wrapped baby gifts of all kinds. In the box, there was also a videotape with a note attached to watch it right away. The tape was of my shower, all my friends were there, talking to me through the camera. I sat watching the tape crying. My son is now eight years old. I'm still far away and miss them all. I still get tears in my eyes when I think of my long-distance baby shower and all my dear friends.

—Connie, Oakland, California

TYPES OF SHOWERS

THE CYBER SHOWER

If the mother-of-honor lives far away, entertain the idea of having a cyber shower. There are several ways to do this. One way is to set up a baby shower Web site for the mother-of-honor that will be up through her entire pregnancy. Then invite everyone to play predesigned games on the home page and to leave their congratulations. You can also e-mail all of your friends with the date and time of the cyber shower. Then set up a private chat room on a particular service, such as Prodigy, CompuServe, or America Online. The host for this "live chat" will have prepared an agenda and activities for the guests. One activity can be Baby Word Scramble, in which the guests have to unscramble a baby-shower-related word—such as *eairdp* (diaper)—which appears on the chat screen. The person who unscrambles the word first is the winner.

The guests can also order gifts from online baby stores and have them shipped directly to the mother-of-honor. Today it is even possible to order virtual flowers and e-mail electronic greeting cards. Use your imagination. The cyber sky is the limit!

THE SECOND, THIRD, FOURTH . . . BABY SHOWER

Some folks believe that it is inappropriate to give a baby shower after the first baby is born. The fact is, every child, every pregnancy, every delivery, is different and each baby deserves his or her own special welcome. So go for it!

You may find out that the mother didn't have a shower for the first child's birth and always wanted one. But what gifts do you give a mother who may still have most of what she needs from the first baby?

There are always new gadgets on the market you can purchase for the mother and the child, such as nanny-cams (video cameras in the teddy bears). Other things moms-to-be always need are diapers, wipes, baby furniture, toys, and cloth diapers to protect mothers' clothes when burping.

Also, don't just assume that because the mother already has one baby the baby clothes are usable for the new baby. Food stains and normal wear and tear can limit hand-me-downs for the new baby. Besides, it is always nice to have some new things for the new baby.

If the mother truly has everything she needs for the baby, which is rare, ask the guests to bring their favorite children's books and to write something personal in them so the baby will have a personalized library.

Another favorite is to have the guests bring a ready-to-freeze dish, which will be eaten after the baby is born. This helps Mom after bringing the baby home because she won't have to cook and can spend more time recuperating. Casseroles and frozen entrees are especially helpful. Even a stack of TV dinners can be a blessing for a harried and exhausted new mom, although fresh food is more appropriate in helping to bring back the mother's strength.

Other gift ideas for a second, third, or fourth baby shower could include:

- Diapers, diapers, and more diapers.

- A gift bag full of diaper rash cream, wipes, diapers, cloth diapers (to be used as burp towels), Tylenol, bibs, baby bath, night lights (for late-night feedings), baby detergent or Ivory Snow, zip-type laundry bags to wash small items like socks.

- Gift certificates to local restaurants that deliver.

- Prepaid house cleaner to come in for a few hours. Arrange to have this done while the mother is still in the hospital. This way, the bathroom and kitchen get cleaned, the dusting gets done, and the laundry and linen will be fresh, too.

- A little basket filled with things to use during the labor and hospital stay. Include a roll of hard candy for Mom to suck on during labor; sample-size bottles of lotion, shampoo, and conditioner; a small tube of toothpaste; and other such goodies that will really be appreciated. Add a few things in the basket for Dad, like a magazine and a calling card for him to use to call family when the baby is born.

- A gift certificate for baby's first portraits.

- A nice picture frame.

- A massage at the local spa for Mom.

- A basket with a CD or tape of romantic music, nonalcoholic wine, a romantic video, massage oils, foot lotion, scented candles, and some fancy chocolates to soothe and rekindle romance for the tired couple after the baby goes to sleep.

When older siblings are involved, remember to bring a small gift for the older brother or sister of the baby-to-be. Small children can get jealous when they spot a ton of gifts for the baby and nothing for them. Cute and inexpensive gifts for the older child include T-shirts or buttons that have sayings printed on them, such as I'M THE BIG SISTER or I'M THE BIG BROTHER (see the resource guide).

Another great gift is an inexpensive camera made for children that takes real photographs, such as the Fisher-Price camera. Large drug store chains also carry small cameras made just for children, or you can purchase a disposable camera and wrap it up. The big brother or sister can use the camera to take photographs at the hospital or to photograph the arrival of the new brother or sister.

Gifts that foster responsibility in the older child are great, too. Dolls and small pets (ask the parents for permission first) help the child understand the principle of caring for something. Another idea is to have a separate cake made that is decorated with "I'M GOING TO BE A BIG BROTHER/SISTER." The icing can include the child's name.

Also plan to give a gift to the older child from their new baby brother or sister and have a gift from the older sibling to the new baby. This encourages bonding and imparts a special sense of connectedness and belonging.

There are great African-American books on the market for a child who is about to become a big brother or sister. Some of the classics include the following:

- Everett Anderson's *Nine Months Long* by Lucille Clifton
- *She Come Bringing Me That Little Baby Girl* by Eloise Greenfield
- *Sweet Baby Coming* by Eloise Greenfield
- *Baby Says* by John Steptoe
- *My Mama Needs Me* by Mildred Pitts Walter

All of these will help to keep the older sibling from feeling left out and from becoming jealous. The more you involve the siblings in the shower, from the planning through the activities, the more they will feel part of the family and the larger African-American community.

THE SHOWER FOR THE ADOPTED CHILD

When hosting a shower for a newly adopted baby, it is vitally important to treat the adopted mother the same way you would treat any new mother.

It is often a good idea to wait until the baby arrives to host the shower, just in case the biological mother changes her mind or something goes wrong with the paperwork. Even if the adoptive parents have a great relationship with the birth mother, it may be too painful for her to sit through a shower for her own baby, so don't invite her unless she or someone else requests it.

Remember, the adoptive mother will need the same baby items that a biological mother will need, so don't plan to shop any differently.

Psychologically, it will be best for everyone involved if a sense of family and community is imparted to the mother and the child right from the start. Always be thoughtful. Avoid awkward or insensitive remarks, such as "I'm sure she'll be just like your real daughter in no time."

THE SHOWER FOR TWINS

When the mother-of-honor expects to be doubly blessed, be sure to note on the invitation that the prospective parents are anticipating the birth of twins. Most people won't mind doubling up on the gifts when they know twins are involved.

It is easy to combine the twin theme in your shower by using a Noah's Ark motif and putting on the invitation, "THEY'RE COMING TWO BY TWO" OR "I THINK WE COULD USE AN EXTRA PAIR OF HANDS . . ." The shower cake could even read, "DIAPERS AND PINS: YOU'RE HAVING TWINS ! ! !"

THE DOUBLE SHOWER

When two women in the same family or two friends are pregnant at the same time, sometimes a double shower is held. A double shower is one shower for both women. This is usually not a good idea. A double shower can cause friction and even ruin relationships. (Besides, it looks cheap!)

Each pregnancy is unique and should be celebrated properly. When a double shower is being considered, it's always best to ask the mothers-to-be. You will probably find that they really would like to have their showers separately.

This is also better for the guests who will attend both showers. It can be a financial burden to have to purchase two gifts for one shower. But if you have separate showers, and schedule them at least one week apart, the guests can budget their money better. Otherwise the guests may be forced to split the original gift budget in two. This can cause guilty feelings and resentments, which never make for a festive occasion.

THE DADDY SHOWER

If the mother is willing, you may consider holding a separate baby shower just for Dad. After all, he is experiencing this pregnancy and birth, too. Couples are surprised to find that the new

A Blessed Event

Gary's co-workers at a radio station in Philadelphia decided to give him, along with another new father, a daddy shower. The new dads were surprised to walk into a "meeting" only to find all of their family and friends gathered together to celebrate that most blessed event—the birth of a new baby. As they walked bewildered through the conference room door, they wondered what was going on. They had never heard of a daddy shower and had no idea what to expect. The host greeted them with pink and blue hats and a giant pacifier, which each wore around his neck. Gary recalls;

"I was stressed out from Lisa's pregnancy, and my daddy shower gave me an emotional boost. It created a real, solid family atmosphere and bonding before the baby was born. In ancient days, the mother was just wheeled to the delivery room and the father was left out. Today the father is an intricate part of the pregnancy and delivery. This type of shower helped me feel more connected and involved right from the beginning."

dad's friends are often excited about going to a daddy shower. Most men, because they traditionally haven't attended baby showers, don't know what to bring. This is where the women come in. Men, generally, don't like to shop, and they will often give money instead of a gift. Money, of course, is a great shower gift because it enables the parents to buy whatever they need. Though money is a great gift, assisting the guys with gift purchases can easily be resolved by notifying them of a gift registry.

It's also a good idea to suggest gifts to men. (Or you could end up with just about anything—electric trains, footballs, and a skateboard.) Often with men, it's best not to leave it to their imaginations. One guest of a daddy shower brought a six-pack of bottled beer wrapped in a ribbon with different-colored baby bottle nipples on the tops! For instance, have all of the guys bring different sizes of disposable diapers. This way the new parents won't have to worry about diaper purchases for a few months.

Just for Dads

As a centerpiece for the father's table, get a basket and fill it with all the necessities he will need to perform his new job. Some examples:

- film
- No-Doz
- financial magazines
- cue cards for the delivery room (PUSH, DON'T PUSH, BREATHE, DON'T BREATHE, I LOVE YOU!, WHAT DID YOU SAY???, and, DO YOU LOVE ME?! are musts!)

For a daddy shower, you can also make it a barbecue or a pizza-and-beer party and invite his friends and relatives. Using a theme or gimmick, such as a poker party, bowling tournament, or a sporting event, can also guarantee the shower's success. You may find that it works best to hold a daddy shower at his job. Because the new father and mother often work at different places, they usually have different friends at their jobs to share in this blessed event. This gives different groups of friends and acquaintances a chance to attend your shower, and no one will feel left out. Be creative, and don't forget the cigars!

THE COUPLE SHOWER

Should we invite Dad, too?

Well, if he wants to come, by all means let him. He was there when the baby was conceived, wasn't he? Isn't he having a baby, too? Dad should be there if he so chooses. But many men feel funny or awkward about attending showers. Others may feel as if they're intruding at a function that traditionally falls in the women's domain. So it shouldn't be considered mandatory if the father doesn't want to attend.

However, if the father attends, it's necessary to let him participate in the celebration. Give the father a contemporary shower hat to wear along with the mom's traditional one. The father can take part in all of the activities or he can be asked to be the master of ceremonies. He can also share in the opening of the gifts and the videotaping or taking of photographs of the event. It's also a nice gesture and makes for a fine tradition if Mom and Dad exchange gifts with each other at the shower and at the adoption or birth of every child. Another suggestion is for Dad to be given a MOM-IN-TRAINING or COACH T-shirt and a stopwatch, to time the contractions and otherwise help in the labor room.

THE CREATIVE SHOWER

Some creative people may choose to adopt a theme and include costumes, which may focus on a period of history (such as a Seventies Shower) or cultural aspects (an African or Roots Shower). Theme showers present unique opportunities to explore our African-American traditions. Along with the costumes, activities, decor, party favors, and gifts can all play a role in a theme shower.

Use your imagination. Know your mother-of-honor's likes and dislikes and plan accordingly. A baby shower is a community celebration as well as an intensely personal rite of passage, especially for first-time mothers.

By invitation only

◎ BY INVITATION ONLY

Who is to be invited? This is one of the most significant elements in planning a successful baby shower. In Africa, people are invited to special celebrations by word of mouth, but in this country, shower invitations are expected. An invitation should arouse curiosity and begin the excitement of the party ahead of time. The invitation should make people even more interested in coming to your party. An invitation can be written formally or given over the telephone. Just remember to give the basic information of who, what, when, and where. Telephone invitations are appropriate for small get-togethers, but for large groups, use written invitations.

Written invitations can become particularly difficult if the shower is to be a surprise, because the invitation is evidence that there is going to be a party. If it is to be a surprise party, it is necessary to collaborate. Discuss the plans with the appropriate people, usually the baby's father and the mother's family. They may be able to help you prepare the guest list.

If that's not possible, try to acquire the expectant mother's telephone and address book. Be sure to ask her permission, or if that will give away the surprise, ask a family member or other loved one. (No one likes his or her privacy invaded, and it could cause awkward moments.) The address book can be invaluable in making the guest list. Even if you know the guests, it can save a lot of trouble simply by providing you with the proper names and addresses of friends and relatives.

Be sure to let the guests know that the shower is to be a surprise. You don't want them to accidentally spill the beans. Also, be careful not to leave any evidence of the invitations around for the mother-of-honor.

If it is not a surprise shower, ask the expectant mother for a list of guests she may want to invite. She may prefer to be involved with particular stages of the planning and preparation.

At the shower, invite older members of the family to sit in the front area of the room. In Africa, this is done as a gesture of respect. Since baby showers traditionally involve the womenfolk, let everyone know whether to bring children along. If the mother-of-honor doesn't mind, it's best to plan activities for children. It is also a good idea to have a teenager present to assist with babysitting and children's activities.

Quill and inkwell

Ways to Surprise the Mom-to-Be

Just a word of caution: Keep the surprise to a minimum. A sudden shock could send the expectant mother into labor before the shower!

- Several days or a week beforehand, make plans with the mother-of-honor to go shopping. What expectant mother doesn't love to look at all the nice new baby clothes and toys!
- Take the mother-of-honor out for a cup of tea or to a juice bar, and make sure you don't return until the guests have had time to arrive and prepare.
- Take the mom-to-be out to dinner or to a play. Tell the guests to be punctual so that when you return home, everyone will already be assembled for the surprise.
- Arrange for one of the guests to use public transportation. Preplan to have the parent-of-honor meet the guest at the airport, train, or bus station. This will give the host some preparation time to set up the baby shower.
- Host the party at someone else's house and just happen to stop there with the mom-to-be.
- Host the party at an African art gallery or a restaurant, and tell the guest-of-honor that you are treating her to a night on the town.

African birth traditions: In Ghana, the men are invited to the mother's home for the ceremony, and the women prepare the food for the event. In the afternoon, drummers and musicians perform, and both men and women dance together in celebration.

THE INVITATIONS

There are several different Afrocentric baby shower cards and invitations that can be purchased in stores (see the resource guide). Hosts can also be creative and make their own. It is always a good idea to make sure your invitations follow the shower theme.

One sister-friend made an invitation on a computer. She found a piece of clip art featuring an African-American baby, and she typed all the pertinent information about the party on it and wrapped it in a newborn-size baby diaper. She mailed them in waterproof white envelopes.

Another sister took her ultrasound picture and scanned it into the computer. She then used it as the front of the invitation. The caption said, "This baby is growing fast and getting ready to make an appearance." A cute idea for another computer-generated invitation is to use morphing software to predict what your new baby will look like. To do this, you need a photo of the mom-and pop-to-be. The photos are scanned into the computer, blended together, and morphed into a young child. It can be either a boy or girl. Once you have your morphed photo of your new baby, put it on the front of your invitations with a caption such as "Baby Jones at Ten Years Old—Year 2011. Come Welcome Him/Her to This World on March 3, 2001." One creative couple took the morphed photo and had the face scanned onto a cloth doll with a diaper and wrote the invitation on the belly.

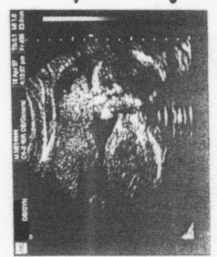

Ultrasound invitation

There are lots of possibilities for invitations. Instead of morphing the pictures, just use the mother and father's baby pictures on the front of the invitation and write, "They're Expecting." Or you can photocopy a birth certificate. Instead of the usual statistics, you can replace them with party details and directions.

Other possible invitation sayings include these:

A Blessed Event Is in the Making
A Pre-Labor Day Celebration
Luv Made This Happen
We've Been Blessed

Also try using African proverbs that pertain to motherhood on your invitations, to keep with the Afrocentric theme.

Be sure to mail invitations at least two weeks before the event. It is also acceptable to send them sooner, up to four weeks prior to the shower. When inviting guests, remember the rule is that only 80 percent of your invited guests will show. Therefore, if you invite thirty guests, you should expect twenty-four to attend.

Including a self-addressed, stamped postcard to make the RSVP convenient will increase the response rate and won't put pressure on guests to make up excuses to explain why they can't attend. Be sure to also include a map card with clear directions to the shower location. Don't forget to enclose information about the gift registry, if available. Inform and remind guests of any items required for participa-

tion in activities. For example, if guests are expected to bring baby pictures of themselves for a shower game, or if they must bring a memento to add to the baby's time capsule, then include the request with a brief explanation in the invitation. If there are various items needed in order to participate in the variety of shower activities, provide a list of needed items as in a scavenger hunt. For instance, include a suggested item for the time capsule, a cassette tape of a song that can be sung to a baby, and a baby photo. The person who arrives with the most items on the scavenger list wins! This way the fun starts before the party.

Party scene

DISTINGUISHED DECOR

There are various commercial decorations on the market for baby showers, but finding decorations for an African-centered baby shower can be a difficult task. A parent or hostess could end up traveling from one gift shop to another to find the appropriate decorations. This section will identify many of the resources a hostess will need to have the perfect African-centered baby shower.

Most of the decorations discussed here will be homemade. There are various weaves of Kente material that are designed for specific occasions. The Kente cloth shown in the accompanying illustration is traditionally used to celebrate the birth of a new baby. This sacred cloth marks a rite of passage, a time in a person's life when a new stage is entered. Don't feel that Kente cloth is your only option for decorations. The continent of Africa is so diverse you can find a wide variety of designs used in ceremonies and everyday life by people from its various countries and cultures. There are ready-made designs you can copy in the appendix of this book.

Mother-of-Honor chair

SYMBOLS

Specific African Adinkra cloth symbols are depicted and described on pages 76 and 77. These may also be used in creating the African decor for the party. There are also various Kemetic symbols from Egypt that are befitting the birth of a baby. These designs can be found in many books about Egypt and its cultures, which identify, discuss, and describe Kemetic symbols.

MOTHER-OF-HONOR'S CHAIR

The mother-of-honor should be provided with a special chair or stool.

Wicker hat with bows

A simple way to prepare an African seat-of-honor is to decorate a wooden chair with raffia and cowry shells on the ends. It takes little time to make a mudcloth cushion for the seat.

For a special effect, try hanging a Kente umbrella from the ceiling with African fertility doll cutouts hanging from the edges.

CENTERPIECES

BIG BABY BOTTLE

Decorative centerpieces are limited only by your imagination. Try filling baby bottle banks (found at Toys "R" Us or your local baby store) with your favorite candies. Tie ribbons around them, add paper flowers, and tie balloons to them for delightful decorative centerpieces.

Wrapping Paper and Bows as Mementos

When opening the gifts, ask a creative person to make the traditional paper-plate hat from a wicker paper-plate holder. This will contribute to the natural theme. It is quite easy to make a wrapping paper corsage by folding the petals and using pipe cleaners or wire trash bag ties as the stem. Save all of the ribbons and bows that come with the presents to make a pretty wreath for the infant's bedroom door.

WRAPPING PAPER CORSAGE
- · scissors
- · green pipe cleaner or wire trash bag ties
- · wrapping paper and ribbons
- · pins

Take a variety of colors of wrapping paper and fold it in an accordion fold. Then, keeping it folded, fold it in half. Wrap the tip of a pipe cleaner around the middle of the fold. Just add ribbons and then open the folds of wrapping paper and pin it on the mother-of-honor. It's also nice to make smaller or different colored corsages for the guests or as party favors.

DIAPER CAKE

Another favorite centerpiece for baby showers is the diaper cake. To make one, open a package of diapers, and roll them together until you get a big circle. Use Scotch tape to hold them together. Use ribbons for the icing and decorations, or purchase a cake topping featuring a baby or shower motif from the craft store.

Diaper cake

African fertility dolls

AFRICAN FERTILITY DOLLS

There are a variety of sizes and designs of African fertility dolls available on the market. African fertility dolls are often placed around the room of a woman who may be having trouble conceiving a child to increase her ability to have children. These dolls are usually small and have a flat or disk-shaped head. The bodies are usually straight with nubs as arms. They can be elaborately decorated with hundreds of beads or simple woodcarvings. There are also a variety of other woodcarvings from Africa that show the splendor of motherhood. Use natural materials such as raffia and flowers to decorate the statues. They make a precious centerpiece and a memorable gift.

PLANTS

Green plants can make the most spectacular decorative centerpieces. They are especially meaningful if they utilize an African motif. Ask a florist to design a centerpiece using flowers and plants from Africa.

Plants and water represent life. Plan to have at least one plant available in order to pour the ritual libation into it (water poured into the plant in honor of African ancestors) before the guests begin eating.

BALLOON BOUQUETS

It is easy to make your own balloon bouquet, but it is also possible to purchase balloon bouquets from a florist or specialty shop. Here, too, you can ask the florist to use an African motif.

BALLOON RELEASE

Hang a net full of balloons over the door. When the mother-of-honor walks through the door, release the balloons.

TEDDY BEAR AND AFRICAN DOLL CENTERPIECES

A doll or teddy bear centerpiece can be made by purchasing a large doll or teddy bear and a smaller doll or teddy bear. Wrap the large mother with African fabric like a dress. Also wrap the mother's head with a fabric headwrap. Or tie a paper flower to the mother bear's head with a piece of ribbon.

Then take the smaller doll and tie it to the mother bear's back in a sling. (In West Africa, the sling is called a *pagne.*) The baby can also be dressed or decorated like the mother. Or try wrapping the baby under the mother bear's dress to make the mother bear look pregnant.

Stand the dolls up using a doll stand (which can be purchased at a craft store, or make a stand with a wire coat hanger). Of course, any type of stuffed animal can be substituted for the dolls or

More Balloons

Make a big balloon pacifier. Hang these big balloons around the room for more baby atmosphere.

· tube balloons (like those used in balloon animal sculptures)
· donut balloons or long balloons
· round balloon

Tie the elongated tube balloon to the end of the round balloon. Then tie the long balloon between the two balloons. If you use a donut balloon, put the deflated balloon in between the elongated tube and round balloon. Blow up the donut balloon last.

Striking decorative centerpieces can also be made using stuffed animals or dolls, cloth, paper flowers, and ribbons.

bears. Since bears are not indigenous to Africa, you may want to select other African animals.

Another decorative centerpiece can be made from an assortment of stuffed African animals. Stuffed tiny or baby animals are often inexpensive. They can be held together with Velcro, or the baby animals can be set in a boat, wagon, or papier-mâché mountain, such as Mount Kenya or Kilimanjaro. With a little imagination, a very striking African centerpiece can be made by just about anyone.

Try making any of these decorative centerpieces or one of your own designs. The more personalized the celebration, the more festive and memorable it will be.

COMMERCIAL DECORATIONS

If you have more money than time and energy, you may elect to use commercial decor. The Beistle Company of Shippensburg, Pennsylvania, sells ready-made African and African-American cutouts for baby showers (see the resource guide).

 PARTY FAVORS

Party favors are, simply, gifts for guests. Be creative with your party favors. Hide some in inconspicuous places, such as in napkins or under seats, or place a sticker on the bottom of someone's plate for a door prize. Have bags of goodies for your guests to take with them to remind them of the party. Remember to purchase or make enough party favors and prizes for the scheduled activities and games. The party favors and prizes need not be expensive. Select one activity and announce that the winner will get the Grand Prize. The Grand Prize, which can be anything, also need not be expensive. A few ideas include a piece of jewelry, cosmetics, or an African doll or carving. A really nice keepsake is to hire a caricaturist to draw the pregnant mom and guests at the shower.

BATH AND BODY FAVORS

Thoughtful and inexpensive party favors are easy to make. Try purchasing a large assortment of lotions, gels, bath beads, and decorative soaps for party favors. Then divide them up equally, wrap them in pretty gold netting, and tie them with raffia. Place one bag at each seat. Women love to get great smelly stuff!

Kenya eggs

KENYA EGGS

In many African cultures, eggs have traditionally symbolized fertility. Kenya eggs are made from beautiful sandstone from Mount Kenya. They can be purchased in many specialty shops and African museums. Put a Kenya egg in a miniature basket and wrap it in tulle. Add a Kente bow and give one to each of your guests.

CHOCOLATE BARS

Chocolate makes a great party favor. Start by purchasing enough chocolate candy bars for all of your guests. Take the outside wrapper off but leave the foil on. Have a piece of African fabric

scanned into a computer. If you don't have one, this can be done by a friend with a computer, or take it to your local printer or copy center. Use this as the background for a new wrapper. Add an African proverb or your own special saying and use a glue stick to seal the wrapper on the chocolate candy bar. Voilà! A beautiful and inexpensive African party favor.

HERBAL TEA FAVOR

Tea is a traditional African gift given to assist the new mother with healing her womb, so it can be a special party favor. Try wrapping pretty packages of herbal teas with a ribbon around the dinner napkins to use as a napkin ring, or design your own unique tea favor.

Other great shower favors:

movie tickets
Afrocentric candles
Afrocentric stationery
Girl Scout cookies
bubble gum cigars
miniature books

AFRICAN-AMERICAN BABY SHOWER ACTIVITIES

When planning to include traditional African-American baby shower games, do not plan too many. Usually, three to five games are enough for one sitting. The hostess can schedule another round of games and activities after the gifts have been opened or after everyone has eaten. This section will provide hostesses with suggestions and ideas for some popular activities and games.

> ### African Party Favor Idea
>
> To make a nice African party favor, purchase some small picture frames that feature African designs. Next, cut an index card to fit the frame, and along the top of the card write, "Coming Attraction." Leave space for a photo in the middle, and along the bottom of the card write, "Little Baby [baby's last name]." Then, when the baby is born, send the guests a birth announcement with the baby's photo sized to fit in the picture frame. You've just made a very memorable Afro-American party favor.

THE OLD WIVES' TALL TALES

Before the party, purchase or make an African animal's tail such as a tiger or lion that can be worn. At the party, on large index cards write several African-American old wives' tales. Write the second half of the expression on the back. Provide each of the guests with a sheet of loose-leaf paper. Read the first half of the old wives' tales aloud. Then ask the guests to confidentially write on the paper what they believe is the second half of the old wives' tale. At the end, the person with the most correct answers gets to wear "The Old Wives' Tail."

Old Wives' Tales

TRADITIONAL AFRICAN-AMERICAN
OLD WIVES' TALES:
- If you dream of fish . . . someone in your family is pregnant.
- If you carry the baby high in the belly . . . it's going to be a boy.
- If your hair falls out and your skin breaks out . . . it's going to be a girl.
- If you let a pregnant woman braid your hair . . . your hair will fall out.
- The person you will argue with the most during your pregnancy . . . is the person your child will most look like.

TRADITIONAL AFRICAN
OLD WIVES' TALES:
- If an animal frightens a woman . . . . the baby will take on a characteristic of that animal.
- If you sleep under the baobab tree all day, your baby will be lazy.
- If a pregnant woman sleeps under a tree . . . evil will come to her baby.

THE BABY LOTTERY

Another excellent African-American baby shower activity finds its roots in the motherland. African women working in the marketplace will hold a lottery among themselves. Each woman will contribute some of her wares or money to the pool. Then they will hold a drawing to see who gets the jackpot for that week. The only exception is if one woman's family is experiencing financial strains, such as the birth of a new child. If this is the case, that woman automatically gets the funds.

In keeping with this cultural tradition, during the baby shower, have everyone chip in a dollar and write down her best guess of what day and time she thinks the baby will be born. The person who comes the closest to the due date wins the lottery pool. Instead of guessing the mother's due date, the guests can guess how many jelly beans are in a baby bottle, or you can use another similar activity.

T-SHIRT ART

Another enjoyable, creative, and memorable activity is having the guests design their own T-shirt for the baby. Simply purchase a baby T-shirt for each of your guests. You can also have your guests pair up to decorate a single T-shirt with fabric paint.

Ask the guests to paint a portrait of what they think the baby will look like. Provide the guests with various paints of skin tones needed to draw an African-American baby. Ask them to write a saying or African proverb on the back of the T-shirt.

Then select someone to judge the T-shirts, and determine the criteria, such as the most creative, appropriate, or interesting. The mother-of-honor can then take the T-shirts home to save or use for the baby.

KARAOKE MOMMA

One of the most enjoyable and hilarious activities is a karaoke competition. Simply ask someone to bring (or the hostess can rent) a karaoke machine. On the invitation, ask guests to bring a tape that could relate to having a baby, such as Stevie Wonder's "Isn't She Lovely" or Diana Ross's "Baby Love." Select a panel of judges. The hostess can then ask the guests to perform. This can also be done with a favorite or hit song. The winner gets a prize or party favor.

Baby block scrabble

BABY BLOCK SCRABBLE

Purchase at least four sets of wooden alphabet blocks and a timer. Mix them up on a table in the center of the room and have the guests gather around. The mother-of-honor picks one person and the timer is set. The chosen guest has to make two baby-type words, such as *diaper* or *formula,* before the timer goes off.

BACK TO BABYHOOD

Another laugh riot can be had by having your guests bring baby pictures of themselves. Then number the backs of the photos and tape them up on a clothesline or piece of yarn. The hostess should pass out ballots and have the guests guess who's who. The winners can be given a party favor. If you are going to use this activity, don't forget to mention on the invitations for everyone to bring a baby photo.

THE PRICE IS RIGHT

To play "The Price Is Right," make a list of baby items and check the prices at a local store. At the shower, ask the guests to guess the cost of baby items. The one who comes closest to the price wins the prize.

BABY ON A PLATE

For this activity, have everyone place a paper plate on his or her head. Then they try to draw a picture of a baby on their head. The person with the picture that looks most like—or anything like—a baby wins.

PIN THE BABY ON THE NEW MOM

This activity is a take-off on "Pin the Tail on the Donkey." Simply trace the mother-of-honor's body onto a large sheet of butcher or wrapping paper. Then cut out several pictures of babies from baby magazines and glue them onto cardboard to make them sturdy. Add tape to the backs of the pictures and play Pin the Baby on Mom. Blindfold the participants, and the guest who gets the baby in the proper place wins.

THE TOILET PAPER MEASURE

For this activity, just have the guests unroll enough toilet paper until they think it will fit around the mother-of-honor's belly. The guest whose "tape measure" is the most accurate wins.

POCKETBOOK PEEK-A-BOO

This game is played by having one person name ten items that may or may not typically be carried in a pocketbook, such as nail clippers, a book, money, a pin, an article of clothing, buttons, and so on. Each guest searches her pocketbook for that item and puts it on the table in front of her. Once the ten items are named, the guest who has the most pocketbook stuff on the table wins.

PREGNANCY PICTIONARY

To play "Pregnancy Pictionary," simply write a list of pregnancy-related terms on a card before the guests arrive, such as *womb, labor pains, baby, episiotomy, maternity ward, Lamaze class, breast pump,* and so on. Shuffle the cards and give each guest one card. Don't let anyone see what is on the cards. Going counterclockwise, one guest at a time will go to the front of the room and draw a picture on a chart pad or on a chalkboard of the term listed on their card. The audience must guess what the picture is that was drawn on the board. The guest who guesses the picture takes the next turn at the board. This is a game where everyone is a winner because it is so much fun.

THE DIRTY DIAPER PIN

Make name tags in the shape of a baby's diaper and fold them. On one of the nametags, squirt a spot of chocolate or mustard on the inside for the dirty diaper. At the end of the games, have the guests open their nametag. The one with the "dirty diaper" wins a booby prize.

CHILDREN'S BABY SHOWER ACTIVITIES

It is becoming more acceptable to invite children and siblings of the baby-to-be to showers. A really nice gesture is for the parents to host a party for the siblings' friends to welcome the new brother or sister. These activities can be used for both types of baby showers.

AFRICAN SAND ART

To make a sand picture like Senegalese artisans do in West Africa from natural colored sands (see photo on page 83), give each of the children an oversize piece of cardboard and white nontoxic school glue. Have the children draw a design on the cardboard and then trace the design with the glue. (Option: Color the sand with food coloring the night before for a variety of colors.) Shake the regular play sand on top of the paper and then pour the excess off. Hang to dry.

Video Blessings

Videotape each guest as he or she contributes blessings for the baby. Get a close-up shot of each guest along with his or her blessing. This makes a nice addition to the video journal. Because the mother-of-honor is usually busy with the activities of the day, she is often surprised to see this very special segment on the videotape when watching it for the first time after the shower.

KIDS SAY THE DARNEDEST THINGS

For this activity, have someone inconspicuously videotape an interview with the children while they are relaxed. Have someone else ask them questions about the baby, such as:

- Where do babies come from? Some funny answers:
  - The stork.
  - Daddy gave it to Mommy.
  - The mailman.
  - The zoo.

- What are you going to call the new baby?
  - A pain.
  - My little blister [sister].
  - I'm not.
  - That's my baby.

- Is the baby going to be a boy or girl?
  - It's going to be a boy because girls stink.
  - A girl because we don't have any toys for a boy.
  - A girl because his shirt is pink.

- How can you tell?
  - My teacher told me.
  - I saw it on TV.
  - Grandma said Mommy's tummy is pointing up so it's a boy.

- If you had all of the money in the world, what would you buy for the new baby?
  - Another family.
  - A pony.
  - All the toys in the toy store.

This will not only keep the children occupied, it can provide great entertainment for the guests.

BABY BRACELETS

Another activity that can keep children occupied and provide them with a memento is to have them make baby bracelets. School-age and older children can string baby bracelets with their names on them. Beads and kits can be purchased from any local craft store.

MARKER MANIA

Provide washable markers and blank paper, and have the children draw what the baby looks like inside the mother-of-honor.

OUTDOOR CHILDREN'S ACTIVITIES

BUBBLES

Buy inexpensive bottles of pink and blue bubbles at the party store for the children to play with outside. Always be sure to provide adequate supervision for all children's activities.

PLAY-DOH OR MODELING CLAY

Cover the picnic or other table with a plastic tablecloth and provide trays for each artist. Then ask them to sculpt a baby or a baby item, such as crib, stroller, or highchair. Let the children vote on which sculpture should be the winner. Provide the winner with a prize, and be sure to give all the children treats or some inexpensive party favors.

Tea Party

To impress your friends, you can have a baby shower tea party. There are companies that will inexpensively cater the ultimate tea party, complete with fine china, real silverware, imported teas and coffees, French pastries, and muffins. To really lay it on thick, hire a harp soloist.

SAND AND WATER TABLE

Purchase two plastic sweater boxes, then fill one with sand and one with water. Provide funnels, tubing, empty squirt bottles, dump trucks, and basters. This inexpensive activity can keep younger children occupied for hours. And it is easy to clean up.

Shower Etiquette Tips

Don't play loud music at the baby shower. It can be very disturbing for both the guests and the mother-of-honor. Soothing tunes are appropriate as background music.

Asking your guests to refrain from smoking at the baby shower is acceptable. It is not healthy for the new mother to be exposed to second-hand smoke.

Don't plan your own baby shower. If you are not sure if your family and friends are planning one, ask them. Recruit your closest family member or friend to be your host and plan it together.

Don't host a shower at a restaurant and then expect the guests to pay for their own meals. The only exception would be if it were mutually agreed upon in a special situation such as an office party. Instead, serve cake and punch if money is a concern.

A baby shower is a time to celebrate the coming of the new baby. There are plenty of upbeat traditions in African-American history to use for a baby shower theme, such as Juneteenth, Kwanzaa, or *Umoja Karamu*; or celebrate various countries of Africa. There are some lesser-known Afrocentric celebrations that make great themes for baby showers:

> A traditional family fish fry.
>
> Mardi Gras.
>
> Ring Shout. An early celebration of African dance with instruments made from animal skin and horns, gourds, tree trunks, and pans. This celebration included a huge feast.

Other celebrations that may be expanded on include:

> Emancipation Day. American abolitionists and free Blacks observed January 1 to commemorate the end of the U.S. external slave trade in 1808.
>
> Pinkster. Observed by the African-American population in Albany, New York, in the mid-1800s, it celebrates the Holy Ghost connecting with each attending guest at the celebration.
>
> Martin Luther King Jr. Day.
>
> Black History Month.
>
> Malcolm X Day.
>
> Savior's Day. An annual holiday observed by the Nation of Islam on February 26 to commemorate the birthday of Wallace Fard Muhammad. The place of worship is decorated with flowers and draped with linens. Gifts and cards are given. Family and friends and the women share a feast and wear white. Speakers are solicited to speak to the guests.
>
> Sorority-themed party.

Congo Square. Blacks gathered in New Orleans in the 1700s behind the city to share African foods, gossip, and news.

Negro Baseball League theme.

Easter Rock. A religious feast in rural Louisiana that mixes pagan and Christian beliefs. A prayer and dance goes on through the night until dawn. Cajun foods are served.

Election Day and Governor's Day. This was observed by free Blacks and slaves in colonial New England. African-Americans would dress up in costumes and fancy clothes to mimic the wealthy white families. They would parade through the streets until dawn.

A Motown celebration theme.

Eid Ul Adha. A Muslim celebration to honor Abraham's willingness to sacrifice his son to honor God. The slaughtering of a goat or lamb is part of the holiday ritual.

Watch Night. Celebrated on New Year's Eve in many African-American churches, where the congregation brings in the New Year praying, singing, and making testimony from dusk to midnight.

If you truly want to celebrate the baby's arrival and don't want to ask someone to throw a party, host a get-together that doesn't require guests to bring gifts.

Never put a request to "bring presents" at the bottom of an invitation. People understand that purchasing gifts is part of a baby shower celebration. It is better to register at a national store and include that information with the invitation, in a brief reminder such as this: "Your presence is present enough, but if you would like to bring a gift, we are registered at . . ."

Don't use computerized address labels on the outside envelope. This is impersonal. Envelopes should be handwritten, or utilize a calligrapher.

Don't use Kente cloth as a runner to walk on. It is a royal and sacred cloth and should be treated with the respect accorded any religious icon or sacred item.

A baby shower is no place for negative emotions.

Don't force folks to participate in activities. If they insist on sitting them out, don't push it. You can include them in other ways, such as asking them to circulate a plate of hors d'oeuvres.

All Wrapped Up

He who receives a gift does not measure.
—*Kenyan proverb*

African people believe that a gift given is only a temporary loss in their budget because sooner or later someone else will return the favor. During celebrations in Ghana, the type of gift you purchase reflects the type of relationship you have with the family. If your association with the family is through the grandparents, then a small present, such as fruit, would be given. But if you are good friends with the family, you may give money and a blanket or a calabash bowl. In America, we also purchase gifts according to how close our association or relationship is with a particular person or family.

However, it is often difficult to determine what type of gift to purchase when a shower is a surprise, especially if the mother hasn't made a gift registry. In this case, enlist the assistance of a family member or close friend to

determine the needs of the mother. It is also possible to ask the expectant mother indirectly what items she needs for the baby without spilling the beans about the surprise shower.

My best advice to all the gift buyers is to be practical and think about who you're buying for: What kind of people are they? What kind of lifestyle do they have? Are there other children or pets to consider? What kind of tastes do they have? If you don't know the answers to these questions, ask. Ask the parents or someone who knows them very well. You'll save yourself—and, more important, the new parents—a lot of time and effort if you buy them a gift they don't have to return.

NATIONAL GIFT REGISTRIES

Most of the national department stores now have a computerized registry. This way, the mother- and father-to-be can walk through the store with a scanner and scan all of the items they want for their new baby. When guests shop at any of the national chains where the parents are registered, they can just enter the mother-of-honor's name into the computer and a list of needed baby items will automatically be printed.

Many of the stores listed in the resource guide include the stores' telephone numbers; however, in most cases, the mother-of-honor must register in person at each store.

Sears kiosk

Daddy's Gift

In some West African villages, as soon as the mother knows she is pregnant, she goes to live with her mother until after the birth of the baby. Meanwhile, the father and his family prepare for the new arrival by building a crib for the baby. When the baby is born, the father goes to the mother's village, bringing with him clothing for the infant and the new mother.

Toys "R" Us
Babies "R" Us
Sears
JC Penney
Kohl's
Target Stores
Wal-Mart

Most national chain stores also have gift certificates available, and they are especially suitable for moms-to-be who live a great distance away.

GIFT IDEAS

BABY'S TIME CAPSULE

If you are the hostess or the mom-to-be, a wonderful idea is to have each of your guests bring an item to put in the baby's time capsule. Suggested items include African-American newspapers and magazines from the day or month of the baby shower, *TV Guide,* baseball cards, a horoscope of the baby's due date (month), a videotape of sitcoms, and pictures of the house or neighborhood where the baby will live.

Always remember to include the shower invitation and other mementos that capture the cultural significance and major local and international events that took place during the year your baby is born.

Be sure to include an item or two from the hospital. For instance, most hospitals provide or sell tiny T-shirts and other items with the hospital logo. Remember to invite the father and the male relatives to send something along for the baby's time capsule. This will be especially meaningful if the newborn is a boy. Men can send along sports statistics and newspapers or magazines with articles about local teams and sports legends.

Wait to seal the time capsule until after the baby is born. This will enable Mom and Dad to add last-minute items, such as family mementos and heirlooms. Plan to open the baby's time capsule as a family event when your child becomes an adult—let's say thirty years from the birth date. It will be amazing for your child to see how things have changed in this period of time.

HERITAGE QUILTS

The making of heritage quilts is a tradition that dates back many centuries. African-American quilts were typically given only for special occasions. In Africa, a special weave of Kente cloth, a regal fabric made by the Fanti people in Ghana, is used specifically in making blankets and quilts to celebrate the birth of a new baby. Also, quilts and blankets are highly prized in many countries in Africa. In times past, blankets were often traded as currency for expensive items.

Enslaved African-Americans were very resourceful. The women often made quilts from old scraps of cloth and clothing. Following in this cultural tradition, after the birth of the baby, hire a quilter to take apart some of the mother-of-honor's maternity clothes worn while pregnant and other familial items to make a memory gift blanket or quilt the entire family will cherish forever.

BABY TRAVEL BAG

Purchase a large diaper bag and include diapers, white disposable bags, tissues, wipes, Q-tips, Balmex, cloth diapers or hand towels, a receiving blanket, a teething ring, toys, Baby Tylenol, sample-size baby wash, shampoo, nail clippers, comb and brush set, face cloth, a small first-aid kit, and a thermometer.

MOM'S GOODY BAG

Purchase an African-print bag with lots of pockets and include a water bottle for Mom, regular strength Tylenol, a small hand-held massager, shower or bath gel, scented lotions, peppermint foot lotion or cream, massage oil, candles, potpourri, scented soap, perfume, warm socks, underclothes, a nightgown to wear at the hospital, pretty hair clips, gourmet tea, a few treats or sweets, and a gift certificate to a salon.

Common and Traditional African Gifts

Many of the traditional gifts given in Africa are gifts that make life easier and secure the well-being of the entire family.

fruit
kola nuts
livestock
beer
baskets
calabashes
tea
soap
clothing
crib
gold jewelry
baby sling
cowry shells
money
pottery
quilts and blankets
religious items and charms

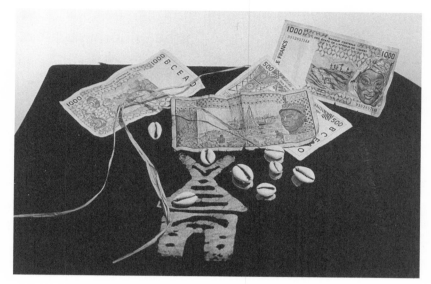

Cowry shells

Other gifts just for Mom:

- pregnancy pillow
- maternity clothes
- T-shirt with the ultrasound transferred on it
- book of African-American sayings or poems about being a parent
- gift certificate for a pedicure, manicure, or massage

A ROYAL SEAT

Traditionally, in some parts of Africa, Ashanti stools (a stool carved from a single piece of wood with detailed, indigenous designs) were presented as a gift to women in order to celebrate the birth of a child. This value of the stool is analogous to the value we today put on a car. People are judged and respected because of the stool. It is considered a seat of honor and power for the wife. The Ashanti

Valuable Shells

Along the Ivory Coast of Africa, women believe that the first present a baby should receive is a cowry shell. This shell represents the spiritual world where the baby came from. Before the French franc was used in West African countries, cowry shells were used as the main source of currency. Each cowry shell at one time was worth 1/8 ounce of gold.

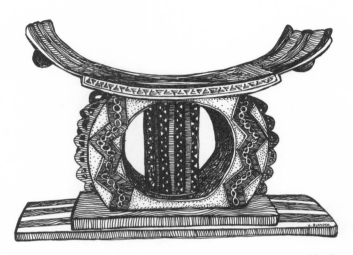

The Ashanti stool shown here is a drawing of the one owned by the Queen Mother of England.

stool is said to be the repository of its owner's soul and is turned on its side when not in use so that no one else can sit on it. There is a legend about the Ashanti stool that can be given to the new mother with the stool. The legend states: "A sorcerer cast a spell upon a cloud, causing it to turn dark and to fill with lightning and thunder and a howling wind. Down from this cloud came a stool carved of wood and covered in gold. It came to rest on the knees of the Ashanti leader, King Osai Tutu. The sorcerer told the king that the stool was the seat that would forever be a symbol of the power of the king and of the life force of the Ashanti people." The sorcerer said, "Let this Golden Stool be carried in processions and used on special occasions. But it must never be sat upon. It will sit upon yet another stool." In the many years that passed, the stool was hidden away, safe from thieves and foes of the Ashanti. Once, when it fell into the hands of Ashanti enemies, the whole nation mourned until its return. Today, the Golden Stool is safely housed in the king's palace at Kumasi, Ghana.

GIFTS FOR THE NEW DAD

The Expectant Father: Facts, Tips, and Advice for Dads-to-Be by Armin A. Brott and Jennifer Ash

David, We're Pregnant by Lynn Johnson

Fatherhood by Bill Cosby

"Poo-Pee" mask, as a gag gift for changing diapers

A mini-getaway weekend for the couple before the baby is born

A ticket to a sporting event

A Child Is Born in Zimbabwe

In Zimbabwe, Juma, a new mother, sends a messenger to her husband's village with the news that their baby was born just two days ago. The father leaves immediately to go visit his wife at his in-laws', and he brings her a copper ring and baby clothes as his gift, which in turn permits him to see the newborn infant.

Meanwhile, the paternal grandparents prepare a basket of food and a cock (if the baby is a boy) or a hen (if the baby is a girl) to take to the wife's parents on the third day after the birth of their grandchild. This is customary, and it is understood that the gifts are a requirement to see the baby. The grandparents won't come unless they can provide these gifts. Many grandparents won't visit the baby for several years until they can afford to provide the required gifts. The womenfolk of the village will bring presents of sugar, meat, and tea to aid the new mother's milk flow.

Forty days later, Juma is ready to go home to her husband's village. Juma's father prepares a pot of sweet beer, a basket of food, and the hen or cock for her to take with her as an offering. When she arrives home, the paternal grandparents will have made a sling for Juma to carry the baby around on her back and a cradle or mat for the baby to sleep on. Juma's husband commemorates the child's birth by planting a tree in their yard.

GIFT BOOKS FOR THE NEW PARENTS

Having Your Baby: A Guide for African-American Women by Hilda Hutcherson and Margaret Williams

Mama Knows Best: African-American Wives' Tales, Myths, and Remedies for Mothers and Mothers-to-Be by Chrisena Coleman

Mama's Little Baby: A Black Woman's Guide to Pregnancy, Birthing and Your Infant's First Year by Dennis Brown, M.D., and Pamela A. Toussaint

BABY-PROOFING KITS

Purchase a good first-aid kit and a general infant health or first-aid book, socket protectors, table bumpers, doorknob protectors, cabinet locks, and faucet pads. Then wrap it all in pastel cellophane paper and tie it up with a big bow.

COMMEMORATIVE BIRTH PLATE

Commemorative birth plates can be purchased at many department stores and specialty shops. Most depict a nursery scene, and you can have the baby's name put on the cradle, the baby's weight at the time of birth on the scale, and the time of birth set on the clock.

The Right Gift

The following are the results of a survey of African-American parents who responded to questions concerning their favorite baby or shower gifts.

Favorite Baby Gifts	Least Useful Baby Gifts
baby sling	bottle sterilizer
lullaby tapes	bottle heater
foot rattles	hand-held rattles
baby album	pacifiers
personalized gifts	wipe warmer
magazine subscriptions	synthetic baby clothes
hand-held vacuum	crocheted blankets
night light	crawling tubes
glider-rocker	cereal bottles
cordless phone	newborn-size clothing
onesies T-shirts	comb and brush sets
cloth diapers	baby jumpers and bouncers
disposable diapers	small diaper bags
large diaper bags	
gift certificates	
bibs	
more bibs	
bathtub seat	
teething rings	
car seats	
stroller	
childproof gates	
maid service for one month	
babybook	
handmade quilt	
quality hand-me-downs	
my first Kwanzaa/Christmas stocking	

AFROCENTRIC GIFTS

There are numerous baby items on the market, and African-American baby items are becoming more and more popular. You can either purchase some of these items or, to give it that special touch, you can make your own. Some Afrocentric gift items available on the market include the following:

- baby rompers with African fabric accents
- terry cloth bibs with Kente designs
- baby buntings with mudcloth fabric
- infant towel sets with African prints
- satin christening gown with Kente fabric

Other Afrocentric gift ideas:

- teddy bears dressed in African fabric (available from Avon)
- African-American baby board books (published by Golden Books and *Essence* magazine)
- soft "Culture Blocks" (made by Cultural Toys)
- African-American dolls (made by Olmec Toys)

AFROCENTRIC GIFT WRAPPING DEPARTMENT

Wrapping gifts Afrocentrically requires imagination and resourcefulness. Wrapping paper can be made by hand or commercial papers can be used. The continent of Africa has a wide variety of cultures and styles. To achieve an Afrocentric effect, try using commercial papers that have bold primary colors (red, blue, yellow) like those used in South African art, the deep earth tones of East Africa, the subtle neutrals of West Africa, and the gentle pastels of North Africa.

Other possibilities include using natural-looking paper that has wood particles in it,

Afrocentric giftwrap

butcher paper, or brown craft paper, like that used to mail parcels and to make paper bags (available from an art supplies store or a packing store). Draw or make a print of Adinkra symbols (symbols used in the fabric made in Ghana for special occasions), use the bold colors of Kente cloth, or create a mudcloth effect with stencils and paint.

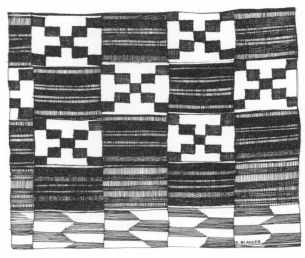

Afoakwa Mpoankron—*Kente cloth pattern used for naming ceremonies*

Kente Cloth

This Kente cloth has a specific weave used when celebrating the birth of a baby. This particular cloth originated from the Earth people of Ghana and is called the *Afoakwa Mpoankron*. The word *Kente* is derived from the Ghanaian word *kenten*, which means "basket." This cloth was originally sold and carried in baskets. Kente patterns have religious, political, and financial significance. The colors are chosen to reflect customs and beliefs.

Try using a rubber stamp of African symbols to decorate the wrapping paper, or make your own. Simple and inexpensive block prints or stamps can be made by carving the symbol from a potato or from a bar of Ivory soap (see page 77).

Try wrapping gifts in baskets and calabashes, and use raffia for ribbon, with natural materials, such as cowry shells and beads, to accent the wrapped gifts.

Akoko Nan
(Hen's feet)

Se Ne Tekrema
(The teeth and the tongue)

Nyame Dua
(God's Tree, or Altar of God)

Adinkra symbols

Adinkra Cloth Symbols

Adinkra symbols are part of a fabric that originated in Ghana. These symbols are numerous and varied, ranging from crescents to abstract forms, and each carries its own significance and represents events of daily life. Adinkra cloth colors used for festive occasions are white, yellow, and light blue.

Akoko Nan ("hen's feet") represents protectiveness, parental discipline, patience, mercy, and fondness. There is a proverb that is associated with this symbol: "If a hen treads on her young ones, it does not mean to hurt them."

Se Ne Tekrema ("the teeth and the tongue") represents growth and interdependence, because as the child grows, the teeth develop and the child begins to talk on his own.

Nyame Dua ("God's tree" or "altar of God") represents the presence of God and God's protection. This symbol has similar representational significance to the cross worn by Christians; it lets everyone know that you believe in a higher power's protection.

THE GODPARENTS

The godparents of the new baby have a special role to play in the baby's life. The baby is officially their responsibility if something happens to the parents, though this is only the case when legally written in a will. It is usually up to the parents, godparents, and the godchild to define the relationship among child and adults. In African communities, godparents don't exist, because if something unfortunate happens to the parents of the child, the entire village takes on the responsibility of rearing and caring for the child.

Make a Block Print

potato or bar of Ivory Soap
carving knife
black ink pad

Cut the potato in half and carve an African design in the cut section of the potato. If you are using soap, carve an African design into the soap. Scrape away the edges from the design so that the design protrudes like a rubber stamp. Test your design on a piece of scrap paper. Then use black, blue, red, and green ink pads to decorate your gift or wrapping paper.

An easy way to get Afrocentric block prints that will last is to take the designs to a printer or stationery store that makes custom stamps. For about ten dollars, they will put the design on a computer and make a rubber stamp.

Making a block print

THE GODPARENTS' ROLE

When choosing godparents for your child, remember that there are specific responsibilities that are part of the godparents' role. Pick people who you trust will carry out their duty throughout the child's life. In America, African-Americans often assign godparents in association with a religious ceremony.

Godparents are expected to:

- represent the godchild by standing in support of him or her at religious ceremonies and rituals.

- remind the godchild of his or her religious background, what that means, and how religion is utilized in everyday living.

- maintain lifelong participation in the spiritual life and religious education of the godchild. This can be accomplished by praying and attending religious ceremonies together, gifts of age-appropriate religious books (such as a child's Bible) and music, and regular contact through visits and letters.

- be available to the godchild as a counselor to offer encouragement and support.

GODPARENTS' GIFTS

Traditionally, the godparents are expected to give specific gifts. The first customary gift is usually the christening outfit. Other appropriate gifts for godparents to give at baby showers are the following:

silver engraved baby cup
a tree to plant
cross on a necklace
first Bible
guardian angel pin
Black-family print by an African-American artist
birthstone jewelry
African-American heritage quilt
savings bonds
stocks

A great gift for parents to give to godparents is *The Godparent Book: Ideas and Activities for Godparents* by Elaine Ramshaw. It is available through Liturgy Training Publications, 800-933-1800.

Shower Etiquette Tips

- Although almost anything goes these days, don't include gift coupons in the invitation that are requests for specific gifts from your guests. Hostesses will sometimes do this to avoid getting duplicate gifts. It is better to register your baby's needs at a national store and include this information in the invitation.
- Don't ask someone to return a gift because you have one already or because you don't like the gift. Save it, take it back yourself and exchange it, pass it on to someone who needs it, or give it to a charity organization like Goodwill.

Birth Customs and Rituals

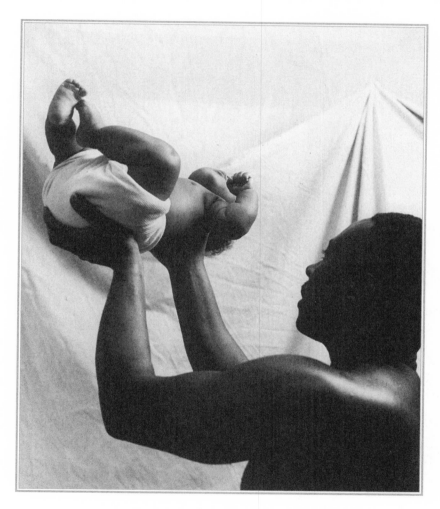

May you bear children like bees!
May you bear children like calabash seeds!

—*Ghanaian parental blessing*

The Birth of a New Child

The woman who has children does not desert her home.
—*Akamban proverb*

The birth of a child is perhaps the oldest and most celebrated event in human history. It is a celebration of the essence of life itself. On the most basic and human level, childbirth is the manifested meaning of life. Procreation has thus always been a cause for celebration in every tribe, ethnic group, community, society, and nation in the world. It is certainly one of the most significant celebrations in the human experience.

In Africa, the significance of motherhood is noted from a girl's first menstruation, which Ashanti women see as the first stage of bringing new life into the world. This is expressed beautifully in a Ghanaian ceremonial prayer offered with a libation by the mother of a menstruating girl:

Senegalese sand painting of mother and child (artist unknown)

Nyankonpon Tweaduapon Nyame [God], upon whom men lean and do not fall, receive this wine and drink. Earth Goddess, whose day of worship is a Thursday, receive this wine and drink. Spirit of our ancestors, receive this wine and drink. This girl child whom God has given to me, today the bara *state has come upon her. . . . Do not come and take her away, and do not have permitted her to menstruate only to die.*

Another example of the profound significance of childbirth in Africa is expressed by the Masai, who regularly hold ceremonies to bless childless women. And if a woman has been unable to conceive for a long time and does become pregnant, the people congratulate the woman with sayings such as "God has taken you from between the teeth of scorners," which implies that childless women are sometimes ridiculed. This is also clear from another Burundi saying, "God has removed your shame!"

While as African-Americans we may not share the same attitude toward childless women, we do share the same sense of pride and joy at the news of a pregnancy. And the birth of a child in African communities is celebrated in a process that begins with the announcement of a pregnancy and lasts long after the infant's arrival in the world.

Motherhood is the most meaningful function for a woman in traditional African communities. In some African societies, a marriage is not fully recognized or considered consummated until the woman becomes pregnant. Special treatment is accorded to pregnant women, and it begins before and continues after the birth of the child.

Although the birth of a child concerns the entire community, this miraculous process is ultimately the business of the mother and the child growing in her womb. This unique bond is also acknowledged by the special treatment accorded to pregnant African women. Other mothers especially share in the sense of pride and joy every new pregnancy brings to the family and the community.

In many African cultures, women must be very careful to observe taboos and certain rules and regulations. These taboos also illustrate the great importance Africans place on childbirth. Some of these are to protect the woman and her infant. Taboos are instituted because a pregnant woman is considered ritually impure. Many taboos concern sexual intercourse, and these vary greatly. Other taboos concern foods that might harm the expectant mother or the infant. One example comes from the Akimba, whose women are forbidden from eating fat, beans, and meat of animals killed with poison arrows. A pregnant woman is also expected to eat the special kinds of earth found on certain anthills and trees. The earth is not bad tasting, and it is thought to strengthen the child's body. Another example is the taboo forbidding work with the use of metal implements, which are thought to attract lightning. Also, the father and mother of an Ingassana infant are forbidden to carry fire before the child is born.

Social taboos are also observed in African cultures. For instance, a pregnant Mao woman can speak to her husband only through an interpreter. This is considered a good way of protecting the expectant mother from any harm—physical, emotional, or ritualistic—that may result from association with her husband during pregnancy.

When a Bambuti woman realizes she is pregnant, she will cook food and take it into the forest, where she offers some in thanksgiving to God. Some African women also wear special protective charms, and some African communities have rituals associated with new pregnancies. Birth customs and rituals in Africa vary as widely as they do on any other continent with a mix of cultures. Some births take place in the home of the mother; many pregnant African women give birth in their parents' home. But the custom of Udhuk women is to go into the forest to give birth. Often a relative will accompany the pregnant woman. After giving birth in the heart of the forest, the mother returns with her newborn and presents it to her husband and family. Most African women squat during delivery. To help relieve the worst labor pains, Wolof women walk back and forth or pound grain on a rock mortar. When a Giyuku woman gives birth, she will scream five times if the infant is a man-child and four times for a woman-child.

The placenta and umbilical cord symbolize the child's attachment to and separation from its mother. Thus they have great ritual significance and are accorded special treatment. Giyuku women, for example, say a prayer for their continued health, strength, and fertility as they bury the placenta in an uncultivated field and cover it with grass or grain. The field symbolizes fertility, strength, and freshness; and the grain symbolizes new life.

African women, like the Ndebele, bury the placenta and umbilical cord under the house where they give birth, so the child is always near its mother, though it promptly begins to grow apart from her.

For many of the same reasons, Didinga women also bury the placenta and umbilicus near the house. Ingassana women put it in a calabash and hang it in a nearby tree. Wolof women bury the placenta in the yard, but the umbicilicus is made into a charm for the child to wear.

The Yansi throw the placenta and umbilical cord into a river, which symbolizes life and continuity. But the ritual has the additional symbolic meaning of showing that the child is no longer spiritual property. It is a member of the community and the world.

In Africa, a woman who gives birth enriches her husband as well as the extended families and community. It is said that "a baby girl means beautiful cows; a baby boy means your name carries on." In the Fulani culture, cows are highly valued and are used as part of a bride's dowry. Male chil-

dren are also desired because they are responsible to provide security and to care for the parents in their old age. But the gender of the child usually doesn't affect the community's attitude toward the baby or its value. The Tsonga and Shangana people of South Africa express the value placed on the sex of the baby through the proverb, "To beget a woman is to beget a man."

AFRICAN BIRTH RITES AND RITUALS

Rites and rituals associated with childbirth vary considerably among the many native peoples of Africa. But they share many commonalities. For instance, most rites and rituals are thought to have a physical or spiritual benefit for the mother, the child, and the entire community. The following examples help to illustrate the complexity and great importance African cultures place on childbirth.

WOLOF BIRTH RITUALS (SENEGAL)

All of these rituals are rich with symbolic meaning and are meant to protect mother and child. After giving birth, the Wolof mother must jump over the fire in the four cardinal directions (North, South, East, and West) before she can sit. The midwife will then hold the child out to her three times. The fourth time the mother is given her newborn infant. Before she suckles the baby, she must give the child a charm that contains a verse from the Koran that has been written on a slab of wood. The verse is supposed to keep away evil spirits. A goat is then killed as a sacrifice, and in the following week a fire is kept burning night and day in the house where the child was born. The constantly burning fire symbolizes the continuation of life. Next to the fire is an iron rod the woman uses to remove the seeds from cotton wool and a pot full of a boiled water plant. The woman drinks from this pot and hangs branches from the water plant over the entrance to the house and uses the compound to protect the baby from any harm.

The knife used to sever the umbilical cord must be kept under the child's pillow. Mother and child remain secluded during this period. If the mother leaves, she must take the knife and leave the stalks of a plant over the entrance. This seclusion ritual symbolizes death and resurrection. But it is also thought to serve a practical purpose as well. In societies with high infant mortality rates, most newborns that die do so within a few days of birth. This seclusion prevents the community from growing attached to the child and from being affected by its death. The knife represents protection and defense against malevolent powers.

FANTI AND ASHANTI BIRTH RITUALS (GHANA AND IVORY COAST)

During pregnancy, Fanti and Ashanti taboos prohibit the father from having sex with his wife, lest the child be born stunted or puny. He is also forbidden from digging in the earth, which is so closely associated with fertility that it is thought that digging in it will kill the mother.

Among the Fanti and Ashanti cultures, the woman is separated from her child, as soon as it is born, for seven days if it's a girl and for nine days if it's a boy.

On the eighth day after birth, a girl child, and on the ninth day, a boy child, is presented to the community and to God. At this time, the child and the mother are reunited and receive gifts from relatives and friends. The naming ceremony is then held for the new addition to the community.

GIKUYU BIRTH RITUALS (KENYA)

Once a Gikuyu woman has given birth, the father will go out and chop down four sugarcanes for a woman-child or five for a man-child. After the juice from these canes is given to the mother and infant, the leftover pieces will be piled on the right side of the house if it's a boy and on the left if it's a girl. Because the right side symbolizes manhood and the left womanhood, every passerby will not only know a woman has given birth, they will know the gender of the child.

After the sugarcane ritual, the infant will be washed and oiled, and if it has been a particularly difficult pregnancy or birth, the father will kill a goat as a sacrifice and call in a medicine man to purify the house.

Among the Gikuyu, the woman is kept in seclusion for four days if it's a girl and for five if it's a boy. During the period of seclusion, only women relatives and helpers are allowed to visit; family members are not allowed to wash in the river; villagers are not allowed to sweep their houses; and no one is allowed to carry fire from one house to another.

After the seclusion period is over, the mother's head will be shaved, and in an act of thanksgiving, the father sacrifices a sheep to God and the living-dead (recently deceased members of the family or community). The woman also makes a symbolic trip into the fields, where she gathers sweet potatoes. Of course, all of these rituals have symbolic meaning. The seclusion symbolizes death to one state of life. This is also symbolized in the hair shaving, where the hair symbolizes pregnancy and must now be shorn, so the new hair, symbolizing new life, can grow in its place.

The hair cutting, like the Yansi ritual of throwing the placenta and umbilicus into a river, has the symbolism of separating the child from its mother and making the child a member of the larger community and the world.

The taboos against washing, sweeping the homes, and carrying fire about the community symbolize the halting or death of the community in anticipation of a new harmony or rhythm of life, which is recognized in the birth of a child. The new child gives new life to the community and adds its own heartbeat to the larger rhythm of life in the community.

THE NAMING CEREMONY

Events follow one another like the days of the week.

—*Tanzanian proverb*

III

seven

What's in a Name?

A good name is rather to be chosen than great riches . . .
—Proverbs 22:1

hat's in a name? For Africans and African-Americans, there is a great deal in a name. In Africa, next to marriage, the naming of a child is considered one of the most significant events in a person's life. In the African tradition, every child must have a naming ceremony. It is only then that the child is separated from the spirit world and is welcomed as part of the family and larger community.

Being enslaved people in America, Africans had their real names taken from them. White slave masters renamed most Africans, and many who refused to take a new name were beaten into submission. The few slaves who were allowed to name their own children knew that as slaves they could very well be separated at any time when one of them was sold to a new master. Consequently, they named their children exclusively after family members or a specific place, not

An Edifying Emblem

A name is an edifying emblem given to a child at birth by the parents or brought from heaven by the child, during that child's birth.

—Reverend Fred Ogunfiditimi

only to honor their ancestors but in a desperate attempt to trace their children's whereabouts in the event that one of them, parent or child, was sold. African children who were named by the slave master often had two names: the registered name given to them by the master and a secret name, or "basket name," given to them by the family. The basket name, like nicknames used today, were usually derived from African words.

Today, after decades of struggle, we have won our freedom, and as African-Americans we now have the right to name our children whatever we choose. Because of this freedom, we often name our children very creatively, with names such as Kanisha, Takita, and Sheria.

Kemetic Symbols

Kemetic symbols originated in the country of Egypt in Africa. These are various drawings or objects that represent gods or life. The word *Kemetic* stems from the Egyptians, who called themselves the *Kmtyw* or *Kemetiu*, which means "Black Egyptians."

Cartouche is one of many Kemetic symbols that originated in Egypt. The oval-shaped sign represents the womb, an individual's personality, and encircling protection. These pendants are often sold as jewelry and can be personalized as a gift with the baby's name.

Lotus Flower is the flower from the lily pad, and it represents the renewal of the spirit and re-emergence of the self.

Ankh is worn as the symbol of life, and it is the original cross. The ankh represents everlasting life, the fusion between male and female energies. It is associated with completeness, eternity, and fertility.

Bess, an Egyptian symbol that was believed to bring happiness to families. This sign is the protector of mothers' children and is associated with joy, imagination, and emotional protection.

Cowry Shells are oval shells that are used in jewelry. This shell, once used as currency, represents wealth, power, fertility, and mysticism.

Yoruba people generally believe the name you give to your child directly affects the child's behavior and that a new name can actually change a child's demeanor. Egyptians believe that an individual does not exist without a name. There is an ancient Egyptian epitaph that states, "Know thyself." Your name is your first identity that propels you toward success in life.

Unlike the American custom, in which the parents usually pick names for the child while the mother is still pregnant, African parents never think of a child's name in advance. Names are often selected on the basis of a significant event, an important occasion, or a meaningful circumstance at the time of the child's birth. Other names signify the occasion of the child's birth. For instance, if it's raining when the child is born, it will be given a name that means "rain" or a name associated with water. If there is a famine, locust invasion, or drought at the time of birth, the child may be given a name that means such events. Still other Africans get names that describe their nature, character, or personality.

Usually, the responsibility of selecting the name for the child is not only with the parents, but the grandparents are included in the decision as well. Grandparents will send, in written form, suggestions for the child's name. Often, the imam (a holy man) or the person conducting the ceremony will choose the baby's name and will be the only one who will know it until the day of the ceremony. During the naming ceremony, after the child's name is revealed, an explanation of the meaning of the child's name is given. Objects that represent the child's name are displayed.

Cartouche

Lotus flower

Ankh

Kemetic symbols

SELECTING AN AFROCENTRIC NAME

Selecting a name for an African-American child should not be taken lightly. There are many different ways that African children get their names.

In African countries, naming a child correctly is so consequential it is said that a baby who is misnamed will cry uncontrollably. This is the baby's way of communicating his wish for another name. Some African villages actually select the child's name while it is crying. As the infant bawls, the parents will recite the names of the child's ancestors. If the baby stops crying when a certain name is called out, it is given this name.

The Mandikas believed that a child named after someone or something would take on seven of their traits or characteristics. Therefore, it is imperative to give the child the name of someone whom the parents admire.

Yoruba families will name a child according to an event that is happening around the time of the baby's birth or the family's circumstances. For instance, a child may be given the name *Bandele,* which means "Traveling" or "A child born away from home." Parents also will give the child a name such as *Italo,* which means "Full of valor," to express their hopes of the type of adult the child will one day become.

In many African societies, God's name is incorporated into the child's name. This is done as a means of praise or worship or to signify that the child is an answer to a prayer. It also illustrates the religious significance Africans place on childbirth.

John S. Mbiti, the Kenyan-born Cambridge professor and author, also notes that the Burundi, Azande, Banyarwanda, and Nuer often invest a child's name with certain characteristics or conceptions of God. For instance, the Burundi and Banyarwanda who want to merge God's might and wisdom will name a child *Ntawuyankira,* which means "No one can refuse Him His way," or they may name a child *Bizimana,* which means "God knows everything."

When they are grateful, they will name an infant *Ndihokubgayo,* which means "I am alive because of Him." Or they might name a child *Ntirandekura,* which means "He has not let me drop

Naming Your African Star

The International Star Registry will officially name an actual star in outer space after your child for a nominal fee. Sisters, let's get busy and give some stars African names! Register your African name or your child's and receive a framable registration sheet, the location of the star, and a map of the constellations. For more information, call 800-282-3333. This is literally a way to have your child reach for the stars and to start him or her on the way to realizing that the sky's the limit.

yet." If they want to express their faith and trust in God, they will name an infant *Niyizbi*, which means "He knows all about it," or *Ndayiziga*, which means "I depend on Him."

The procedures for naming a child vary with different regions of the African continent. The firstborn son can be given part of his father's name to honor his paternal lineage. In West Africa, infants are often named according to the day of the week on which they are born. For instance, a child named *Bosede* was "Born on Sunday." Children are sometimes named to reflect their appearance and are also given names to protect them from evil spirits.

Secret Name

After delivering my son at the hospital, the nurses immediately wanted me to fill out the name on his birth certificate. Since we knew the name, we went ahead and filled out the certificate, but we didn't tell anyone the baby's name until the day of the ceremony. Everyone referred to my son as 'the baby' until his name was revealed.

—Lisa, New York

Among the Akamba and in many African societies, before a ceremony is held and the child is given a name, he or she is considered an object that belongs to the spirits *(kiimu)*. If the child dies before the naming ceremony, the mother is considered ritually unclean and must be cleansed before re-entering the community.

USE YOUR FAMILY TREE

If you are picking a name for your child, you may first want to do a little research to find out if there is an African ancestor or relative whose name you would like to use for your new baby. Unfortunately, due to slavery in America, records of families were not kept accurately, if at all. Therefore, it may be difficult and take some time to research an accurate ancestral African name.

Family Pride: The Complete Guide to Tracing African-American Genealogy by Donna Beasley is a book that can help you to get started researching your heritage. It gives you specific advice in tracing your roots back to Africa. Since most Africans were brought to America from West Africa, more than likely that is where you will find your family's history.

If it seems impossible to trace your history in America back to Africa, adopt a name from a West African family for your child. Since African names are passed on from one generation to the next, there is a good chance that you will be right on target with a West African name.

There are several books on the market on African names and their origins and meanings. Try some of these:

The Book of African Names by Molefi Kete Asante
African Names by Julia Stewart
Proud Heritage: 11,000 Names for Your African-American Baby by Elza Dinwiddie-Boyd
What to Name Your African-American Baby by Benjamin Faulkner

AFRICAN NAMES

Many African families believe in naming a child after an ancestor or a grandparent. In many groups, it is forbidden to name a child after anyone in his or her immediate generation. The child must be named after someone who came before him or her. Here is a sample of names:

GIRLS

Juma *(Jew-ma)*	Born on Friday
Kesi *(Kes-ee)*	Born during financial difficulty
Fatou *(Fa-two)*	Beloved by all
Imani *(E-man-ee)*	Faith

BOYS

Edet *(E-dat)*	Born on market day
Hakim *(Ha-keem)*	Doctor
Kwame *(Kwa-may)*	Born on Saturday
Momadu *(Mom-a-do)*	Popular boy name

AFRICAN NAMES FROM HEAVEN

Ojo *(Oh-joe)*	Male child born with umbilical cord around his neck
Aina *(Eye-nah)*	Female child born with umbilical cord around her neck
Ajayi *(Ah-jah-yee)*	Born facedown, as if praying
Dada *(Dah-dah)*	Born with plenty of hair
Ige *(Ee-gay)*	Born feet first (breech birth)
Taiwo *(Tie-woe)*	First born of twins
Kehinde *(Kay-hin-day)*	Second born of twins
Idowu *(Ee-dough-woo)*	Born after twins

| Ola *(Oh-la)* | Born after Idowu |
| Ilori *(Ee-lore-ee)* | Born of a mother who sees her period throughout the pregnancy |

AFRICAN NAMES RESERVED FOR ROYAL FAMILIES

| Adedayo *(Ah-day-dye-yo)* | Crown becomes joy |
| Aderonke *(Ah-day-wrong-kay)* | Object of royal adoration |

Three Names

Some African names have three parts. The first name is the given name and the meaning is specific to the individual. The second name is the name of the child's father, and the third name is the name of the child's paternal grandfather. Both male and female siblings will share the same second and third names. In keeping the names of their father and grandfather, the children are maintaining their connection to their birth family and ancestors.

In the Dutch and French Guianas, evidence of the African roots in Ghana of the Fanti-Ashanti culture is still seen in the naming of children after the day they were born.

DAY	BOYS		GIRLS	
	Guiana	Ghana	Guiana	Ghana
Monday	Couchai	Kouassi	Corrachiba	Akouassiba
Tuesday	Codio	Kodio	Adioula	Adioula
Wednesday	Couamina	Kouamina	Amba	Aminaba
Thursday	Couacou	Kouacou	Acouba	Akouba
Friday	Yao	Yao	Yaba	Ayaba
Saturday	Cofi	Kofi	Afiba	Afouba
Sunday	Couami	Kouami	Abeniba	Amoriba

BLACK AMERICAN NAMES

Most Black Americans today have a mixture of African and European names that have evolved into unique names, such as LaToya and Dante. This has led to some names that are used more frequently by Black families than by white and are considered to be entirely Black American names. An example of this is seen especially in girls' names that have the prefixes *Sha-* and *La-,* or suffixes such as *-isha* or *-esha* and *-ika* or *-eka.* For example, a name like *Monica* would become *Monesha.* Black parents have been more creative in naming their children than any other group. Inventing new spellings of names and changing standard names like *Sarah* to *Darah* have been seen over the past ten years. You can combine a European name with an African name for your child's naming ceremony. (See Appendix B.)

eight

The Traditional Naming Ceremony

Honor a child and he will honor you.
—*Zimbabwean proverb*

*N*aming ceremonies are ideal celebrations for those African-American families who want to get closer to their roots. As African-Americans, we should be proud to have a name that is African or a combination of African and American. As we have seen in African society, a name is a considerable part of a person's life and a very important aspect of the culture. It is typical to find that in all the various African countries, almost everyone is given a naming ceremony as a baby. It usually isn't an optional event. Much as food is necessary for life, a name is considered essential for a child's healthy growth and development.

We know that names have distinct meanings. A child's name is an edifying emblem that a parent gives to a child. Africans have been performing naming

Naming ceremony: The imam (holy man) blesses the newborn baby.

ceremonies for thousands of years and continue to do so today. During slavery, African midwives kept alive the practice of holding a special ceremony to name a child. Over time, Christian, Islamic, and other religious influences have altered but not halted this most celebrated custom.

The custom of naming ceremonies for African-Americans is relatively new. Our traditions were stolen from us for more than four hundred years, and our religions were forcibly replaced with belief systems that didn't belong to us. In order to maintain our heritage and reclaim our identity, we must look back and acknowledge our past. We then can celebrate our future with a new sense of ourselves and a new sense of purpose.

Far from being just an excuse for a party, a naming ceremony fulfills several momentous social functions besides the naming of the newborn child. It is an important expression of solidarity with the extended family and the community, it offers the older siblings an opportunity to participate in a significant family event, and it is an opportunity to recognize elders, grandparents, and ancestors. It is also possible for absent relatives to participate by sending messages to be read aloud. All of these occurrences mark the commitment of the parents and the entire community.

The traditional naming ceremony is not intended to replace the beautiful sacrament of baptism, which is observed in many African-American communities. Both traditional ceremonies complement each other and can even be performed on the same day. For example, close family members could attend a baptism in church at a morning service, and later in the afternoon, family and friends could gather for the naming ceremony in the home of the parents.

Too often these days, many parents experience difficulty in having their child baptized in church. Some reasons for this difficulty include the possibility that the parents are not married, or perhaps they don't attend that church on a regular basis. It may be that the parents don't have the time to devote to receiving formal baptismal instructions, which are required by some churches. A naming ceremony is not a substitute for baptism, but it is an immediate way for African-American parents and their family members to celebrate and welcome the new baby into the family, community, and world.

Africans and their descendants in other lands often have many names, which they collect throughout life. For instance, the Fanti and Ashanti cultures not only have naming ceremonies during which they name their children after the day they were born, they also take their children to be baptized in church and give them Christian names. To avoid having an "evil eye" (a curse) put on the child, many also take the child to the local imam, who blesses it and gives it a biblical name.

Though it isn't necessary to give your child an African name to have a naming ceremony, it is necessary to share your child's new name with his community. Naming ceremonies give our children the foundation for knowing who they are, where they come from, and who they will become.

Indeed, many African societies believe a child's name signifies its destiny in the world, and names are chosen accordingly.

NAMING CEREMONIES IN OTHER CULTURES AND GROUPS

Besides Africans, there are many other peoples who have traditionally held naming ceremonies for their newborns, including Native Americans, Jews, and Hawaiians.

NATIVE AMERICAN

America's indigenous peoples also celebrate the birth and naming of a child. Like many Africans, a Native American may have several names associated with various life stages. Often the grandparents give the child his or her name at birth. As the child grows, the next name will be based on his or her character.

The Plains Indians, such as the Sioux, the Arapaho, the Kiowa-Apache, the Nez Perce, and many others, often had special naming ceremonies. A few days after a child is born, a festive celebration is held and the child is then given an ancestral name. The child will keep this name until another time is conferred to honor his first great achievement in life. If other children have already received the most highly prized family names, the father or a great warrior from the tribe will name the male baby after one of his war deeds, after something seen in a vision, or after a worthy or courageous animal. Then a singer will report the name to the entire camp and announce that the father or the warrior, in gratitude, will give a horse to a particular poor man in the tribe.

As the ceremony proceeds, the singer announces the family's wish that the infant would live to have his ears pierced. He will also announce that a great warrior or chief will perform the ceremony. Then the tribe vows to protect the child until he is old enough to walk. The ear piercing, which is very painful and done with a sharp stick, will be performed at the first Sun Dance ceremony after the child starts walking.

JUDAISM

Hebrews have held naming ceremonies for thousands of years. It later became the custom to celebrate naming ceremonies in the synagogue. At this time, an infant boy is circumcised. This event is called a *bris*. An infant girl is also named at synagogue at a *brit bat* or *Zeved Ha'bat,* where her father would be showered with candy.

INDIA

In India, an infant is given its name at a naming ceremony called a *Namakarana*. The *Namakarana* is held on the eleventh day after a child's birth.

AUSTRALIA

Australians traditionally hold a naming ceremony on the seventh day after a baby is born. Members of the Australian Federation of Civil Celebrants often serve as masters of ceremonies.

NEPAL

In Nepal, naming ceremonies are held for boys only. In this ceremony, the boy will have his head shaved bald, which symbolizes the start of his journey into manhood.

CATHOLICISM

Roman Catholic priests perform the sacraments of baptism and confirmation for Christian children who are to become members of the Church. Though the Church does not recognize these sacraments as naming ceremonies, nevertheless, when a child is baptized, his or her given baptism and family names are recorded for the Church.

When a child is confirmed, usually at the age of twelve, the child announces the intention to eschew evil and live according to the tenets of the Church. He or she then becomes a confirmed member of the Roman Catholic Church and Christian faith. At this time, the child selects a Christian name, usually the name of a saint or apostle.

Preparations for the Naming Ceremony

However full the house, the hen finds a corner to lay in.
—*Sierra Leone saying*

*N*aming ceremonies usually take place within seven to nine days after the birth of the baby. It is a Yoruban belief that if you do not name the baby within this period, the child will not outlive the parent of the same sex. Since the ceremony is held seven days after the birth of a child, and because it is difficult to predict the day of the birth, it is also difficult to plan the exact day of the ceremony. Most parents begin planning for the naming ceremony when the mother-of-honor is close to birth. Preparations for the ceremony generally begin when the infant is about five days old. First a location must be selected. This ceremony is customarily performed at the parents' or the mother's family home. But it could be held at a hall or in the home of a relative or friend.

One of the first jobs is to invite the guests. The time period between the date of the birth and the naming ceremony is often so short, and it is such a hectic time, that there either isn't enough time or it just isn't possible to fill out and mail conventional invitations. When the delivery date is approaching, friends and family members are usually called on the telephone and verbally put on standby.

When the baby is born, the mother will then call friends and relatives and invite them to the house on the designated day. If planning to send formal invitations, it is best to prepare them beforehand. Upon the child's birth, fill in the date for the ceremony and mail them the same day. If everyone lives in proximity, the invitation should take only a day or two to arrive in the mail. Call all the people invited so they will expect the invitations and prepare ahead of time for the ceremony.

It's a good idea to assign someone to be in charge of securing the entertainment, such as stilt-walkers, singers, drummers, and dancers. Plan ahead and let the entertainers know the due date and ask if they can work with you on short notice.

If the weather is good, the best place to hold the ceremony is out of doors and during the early afternoon. Sometimes naming ceremonies are held on a beach or a mountaintop. Since this is a formal celebration, the house should be decorated with African fabric and flowers. You want to appeal to your guests' five senses. When they walk into the room, there should be interesting things to look at, such as African art, as well as pleasing things to smell, touch, hear, and taste. White candles should be available for each guest to hold during the ceremony. Incense of myrrh can be used to scent the room.

AFRICAN CLOTHING

To distinguish the naming ceremony from other birth celebrations, guests should be asked to wear authentic African attire. Inform the guests of the requested attire far in advance and encourage them to come dressed appropriately. This apparel also sustains the regal atmosphere of the naming ceremony.

The mother should have several outfits available and is expected to change clothes three to four times. She can dress informally for the preceremonial preparations (such as cleaning and cooking), then formally for the naming ceremony. Afterward, she should have a semi-formal outfit for dinner, and then a casual ensemble that is comfortable for socializing and dancing. The father should wear a *grand bubah* and a *kufi*. The baby should be dressed in white. Even siblings should be dressed in their best clothing, preferably of African origin.

GIFTS

At African naming ceremonies, gifts are given for the infant. But the male friends and relatives also bring gifts for the father, and the female friends and relatives present gifts to the new mother.

There should be a decorated gift table available and a cake to celebrate the occasion. Upon the guests' arrival, envelopes with money and food are left on a table at the door as a gesture of goodwill to the infant. In Africa, the guests who bring money for the baby inconspicuously drop the money into the baby's crib for the parents to find later.

CEREMONIAL AND SYMBOLIC ITEMS

A special smaller table draped in Afrocentric fabric is used during the ceremony. It should be placed in a central location. On the table are the following materials that will be introduced to the baby:

- Water. Water symbolizes vitality. The child is as vital to the family as water is to humans.

- Plant. The plant represents life and a place to pour the water from the libation. (If the ceremony is held outside, the libation is poured on the ground.)

- Dirt from the plant. The dirt represents the child's origins, and it is mentioned so that the child will not forget where he or she comes from.

- Silver baby bangle. The bangle represents good health.

- Oil. Oil symbolizes the coming of calm to the periods of hard work in the child's life.

- Salt and sugar. Salt and sugar symbolize bringing improved taste and pleasantness in life. If a person is said to be as salt or sugar to his or her people, it means that person brings joy and sweetness where there is bitterness.

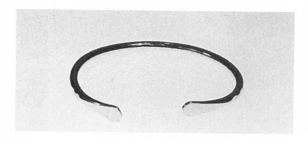

It is believed that the wearing of a silver bangle has healing properties, such as preventing arthritis. Children wear a bangle because it is believed to protect them from illness.

- Kola nut. The kola nut represents longevity.

- Honey. Honey symbolizes the hope that the child will be sweet toward the community.

- Wine. The wine, which can be used in libations, represents bringing happiness to people in hopes that the child will bring happiness to the community at all times.

- A pen. This symbolizes the power of the pen in hopes that the child will be creative, making good things, and not harmful ones.

- A book. The book is usually the Bible or the Koran. It represents a devotion to God and the hope that any position of authority will be used to help others, not to oppress them.

- A large candle. The candle represents a guiding light, which will positively lead the child throughout his or her life.

- Cowry shells or money. These represent wealth and the wish for the child to use his or her wealth to help others.

- Any object that represents the meaning of the child's name.

All of these objects will be introduced to the child during the naming ceremony. They are held before the child and the item is identified verbally. African people generally believe that when the child is introduced to these materials, he or she will make positive use of them and not misuse

them once he or she is an adult. After the introduction of each item, the guests may respond by saying the word *Ashay* (pronounced "Ah-shay"). This is a Yoruban word that means "I agree" or "Right on." It is used much as people use *Amen* at church services.

THE GRIOT

In most cases, family history in African countries has been retained through an oral tradition. Appointing an elder to record your family's history, to act as the official record keeper, can be included as part of the ceremony. This person is called the *griot* (pronounced gree-o). He or she can also be responsible for updating the family tree in the family Bible or Koran.

In the past, the *griot's* duties would include telling true stories about a family through songs. In his stories, the *griot* would be careful not to anger the family by telling an unfavorable story. The *griot* would also play the village "talking drum," which notifies all of the neighboring communities about the birth of the new baby.

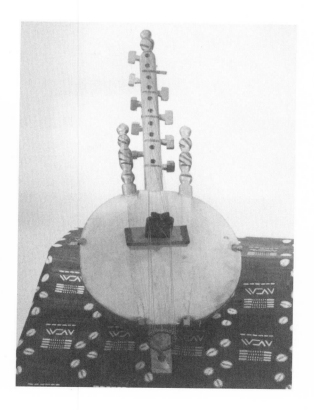

History of the *Griot*

Passing the story of one's family on to the next generation is an African tradition that is still practiced today. African *griots* memorize the genealogy and history of their tribe. The honor of being the village *griot* is passed from one generation to the next.

—from *Family Pride,* by Donna Beasley

The kora *is a musical instrument that is traditionally played by* griots *of West Africa while reciting a song about a family's history.*

It is also customary for the *griot* to recite a song, poem, or story concerning the history of the family at the naming ceremony. Inform your appointed *griot* ahead of time so he or she can come prepared. If possible, have a drummer provide the background beat for the story, or select a recording with an African drumbeat.

THE RITUAL CLEANSING

Before the ceremony, the baby must go through a purification process. Because blood is considered dirty or contaminated, it is believed that the baby became impure during birth. The baby is given a special washing to cleanse him of any impurities. The infant should be held upside down by the feet while being washed. (This practice brings to mind the times when a baby was held upside down by the doctor and slapped on the backside. However, in this ritual, the baby isn't getting slapped, only washed.)

The Naming Ceremony Procession

One family's naming ceremony started a block away from the house where the celebration was to be held. They started a procession down the street with giant African stilt-walkers, dancers, and drummers. The family followed, holding the baby over their heads for all to see. Other members held colorful streamers above their heads. They drew a lot of attention, and many of the neighbors and passersby joined in the procession. (If you are planning to hold a procession or parade to celebrate the newborn baby, be sure to obtain permission from your city to close the street.)

THE FIRST CLOSE SHAVE!

It is also custom to cut the baby's hair as a purification ritual. In traditional African naming ceremonies, the entire head of the baby is shaved. However, there is also an African-American belief, which originated in the South, that it is bad luck to cut a baby's hair before the age of two for fear that the baby's hair will turn "nappy." A happy medium to resolve the clash of these two cultural beliefs is to cut off a symbolic lock of the baby's hair, which can then be saved for the ceremony and for the child's baby book. There is a Senegalese belief that if the baby cries when his hair is being cut, then he will be a generous adult, and if he doesn't cry he will be stingy.

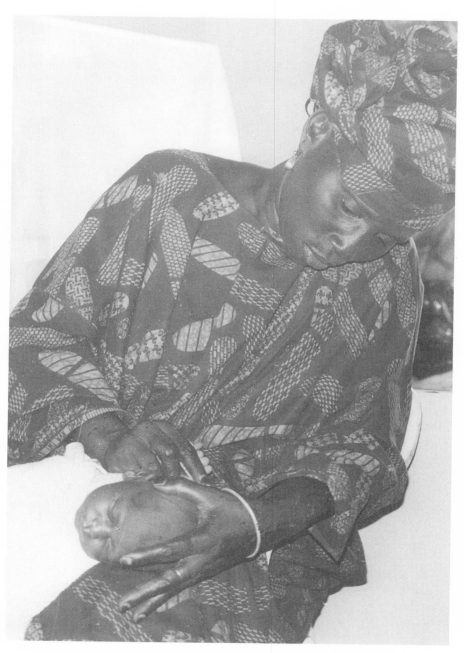

An African woman shaves her nephew's head as a purification rite for the naming ceremony.

t e n

The Naming Ceremony Rites

A child enters the house blindly, but
she comes out with eyes wide open.
—*Mossi proverb*

*T*he naming ceremony is usually held in the afternoon. Family members congregate at the parents' home and celebrate the arrival of the new baby. As they enter the house, each person leaves at the door some small token or gift of goodwill. Some of the items traditionally given are clothing, a blanket for the baby, food, or something for the household.

A loud drumbeat signals the actual commencement of the ceremony. Elders should be seated closest to the event. A female family member, such as an aunt or a sister-in-law, is usually appointed beforehand to carry the baby into the room or to the outside area where the ceremony is being conducted. An imam (or holy man) or a revered family member should officiate at the ceremony.

THE LIBATION

The officiant welcomes the guests and recounts the importance of why they have gathered together. The commencement libation is poured into a

111

plant from a wooden unity cup and a prayer is offered. Water is often used in the commencement libation to symbolize the new life. Later in the ceremony, other liquids can be used for the libations.

LIBATION PRAYER

As we gather here today, we ask that God and our ancestors watch over us and our families. We ask for their blessings as we pour this libation in their honor to the East [always start the libation in the direction of the African continent], West, North, and South of us. Amen.

THE UNITY CUP

The Unity Cup is used specifically in African ceremonies to pour libations. This cup is used in African-American ceremonies, such as Kwanzaa, and is usually made from natural materials such as wood, stone, or the mud of pottery.

The officiant also asks the spirits of the family's ancestors to be with them on this day. The libation is poured into the soil of the plant or on the ground to represent those who came before us who are now buried in the earth, represented by the soil in the plant. While the libation is pouring, the officiant says a short prayer while facing each of the cardinal points, first East, then West, North, and finally South. This gesture is to include all ancestors, wherever they may have lived.

Unity cup

Other libation liquids may be poured for various reasons, such as in gratitude or in prayer for the health and welfare of the infant (see the section on libations on page 9).

THE ANNOUNCEMENT OF THE SELECTED NAMES

All of the names that have been offered by family members are then announced, along with the meaning of each name. However, the actual name of the child is not yet revealed. The reading of personal messages sent by relatives living too far away to attend the ceremony is also done at this time.

THE LIGHTING OF THE CANDLE

As the parents light the large or central candle, which is the symbolic light that will guide the child through life, the officiant whispers the chosen name in the baby's ear three times.

The child is the first one to hear his or her own name spoken. The Mandinkas believe that each human being should be the first to know who he or she is. The significance of this act is to separate the child from the spirit world where he or she is considered only an object. This exercise marks the child's official entry into the family lineage.

The parents then announce the baby's full name to the guests. They tell how it was chosen, and they give its meaning. They begin by saying, "I now present _____ ..."

PRESENTING THE CEREMONIAL ITEMS

As the parents and guests stand close by, the officiant cradles the baby in his or her left arm, announces what each symbolic item stands for, and touches the various items to the baby's lips with his or her right hand so the baby can taste them. Some of the items will be bitter and some sweet; this represents the bittersweet journey of the life the baby will soon experience. As the officiant is touching each item to the baby's mouth, he or she also explains the symbolic meaning of each item to the guests.

THE SYMBOLIC FIRST STEP

After all of the objects are used, the officiant then takes the baby's bare foot and touches it to the ground. This symbolizes that the baby's first steps will be in the right direction.

The Pygmy Dedication Rite

Women express gratitude to God after childbirth. They believe that life comes ultimately from the Creator and is sustained by God. The following prayer is said by Pygmy women in a ceremony of dedicating a baby to God. The mother and father lift the baby toward the sky and pray:

"To Thee, the Creator, to Thee, the Powerful, I offer this fresh bud, new fruit of the ancient tree. Thou art the Master, we Thy children. To Thee, the Creator, to Thee, the Powerful: Khmvoum [God], Khmvoum, I offer this new plant."

—from *The Role of Women in Traditional African Religion* by John Mbiti

Religious Verses

BIBLE VERSES ABOUT CHILDREN AND PARENTS

Children, obey your parents in the Lord: for this is right. Honor thy father and mother, which is the first commandment with promise; that it may be well with thee, and thou may live long on the earth. And, fathers, provoke not your children to wrath: but bring them up in the nurture and admonition of the Lord.

—Children and Parents, in Ephesians 6:1–4

And they brought young children to him, that he should teach them: and his disciples rebuked those that brought them. But when Jesus saw it, he was much displeased, and said unto them, Suffer the little children to come unto me, and forbid them not: for of such is the kingdom of God. Verily I say unto you, Whosoever shall not receive the kingdom of God as a little child, he shall not enter therein. And he took them up in his arms, put his hands upon them, and blessed them.

—Jesus Blesses the Little Children, in Mark 10:13–16

Hear, ye children, the instruction of a father, and attend to know understanding. For I give you good doctrine, forsake ye not my law. For I was my father's son, tender and only beloved in the sight of my mother. He taught me also and said unto me, Let thine heart retain my words: keep my commandments, and live. Get wisdom, get understanding; forget it not: neither decline from the words of my mouth. Forsake her not, and she shall preserve thee: love her, and she shall keep thee. Wisdom is the principal thing; therefore get wisdom: and with all thy getting get understanding. Exalt her, and she shall promote you: she shall bring thee to honor, when thou dost embrace her. She shall give to thine head an ornament of grace: a crown of glory shall she deliver to thee. Hear, O my son, and receive my sayings; and the years of thy life shall be many.

—Parental Advice, in Proverbs 4:1-10

KORAN VERSES ABOUT CHILDREN AND PARENTS

Your Lord has decreed that you shall not worship except Him, and your parents shall be honored. As long as one or both of them live, you shall never say to them, "Uff" [the slightest gesture of annoyance], nor shall you shout at them; you shall treat them amicably.

And lower for them the wings of humility, and kindness, and say, "My Lord, have mercy on them, for they have raised me from infancy.

—The Night Journey, 17:23–24

THE LIGHTING OF THE CEREMONIAL CANDLES

We enjoined the human being to honor his parents. His mother bore him arduously, gave birth to him arduously, and took intimate care of him for thirty months. When he reaches maturity, and reaches the age of forty, he should say, "My Lord, direct me to appreciate the blessings you have bestowed upon me and upon my parents, and to do the righteous works that please you. Let my children be righteous as well. I have repented to you; I am a submitter.

It is from these that we accept the righteous works, and overlook their sins. They have deserved Paradise. This is the truthful promise that is promised to them.

Then there is the one who says to his parents, "Woe to you; are you telling me that [after death] I will come back to life? How come those who died before us never come back?" The parents would cry for God's help and say, "Woe to you; please believe! God's promise is the truth." He would say, "Tales from the past!"

—The Sand Dunes, 46:15–17

Guests are asked to light their candles from the main candle. At this time, a traditional African prayer is offered and a Bible or Koran reading is recited.

THE ORATIONS

The officiant then offers a prayer. The parents or *griot* are then asked to offer a prayer, poem, story, or speech.

African Naming Ceremony Poem

To have a child is to have many blessings.
God handpicked this child just for you from heaven.
Take great care of your child and this child will take care of you.
Child, may your parents always be proud.
Though this infant has just arrived, his [her] path has already
   been set.
This child you see before you is destined for many great things.
Child called [baby's name], may this name dwell in you.
This baby born into our family is part of our community.
Parents, friends, and everyone here are responsible for his [her]
   care because it will take this village to raise this child.
Let's wish our new addition long life in comfort and good health.

THE PRESENTATION OF THE CHILD

The father then announces the name of the child once more while raising the infant overhead. Each guest is asked to touch the child during this time and to offer his or her own individual prayer or blessing.

THE BENEDICTION

Close the ceremony with an appropriate benediction. After the closing of the ceremony, some
African and African-American parents dedicate a
tree sapling with silver naming ring around the
tree's trunk. As the tree grows, the ring gets perma-
nently embedded in the trunk. This dedication is an
enduring reminder of the celebration that just took
place. Festive music and dance are appropriate
thereafter.

African-American Music

Music to African people is not
specifically for a special occasion, though
there are special events, like naming ceremonies, where dancing and singing are
appropriate. Music has always been an inspirational outlet for Africans, so much
so that slaveholders thought that Africans
loved servitude because they were always
singing, whether for sorrow or celebration. No matter what the event, there is
always a song to fit the occasion. In the
beginning there was music. First there
were the Egyptians who were well known
for their famous trumpet blowers; then
there was the sound of the African drum
rhythms through the jungles of the
motherland, which created the beat for
the womenfolk to dance. The Negro spir-
ituals then provided an outlet to remember the motherland without persecution.
Today we have jazz, rhythm and blues,
blues, and gospel. Any of these types of
music can be played during your celebration to provide a cultural accent for this
special event.

African instruments: kora (top), *balaphone*
(left), *and goatskin drum* (right)

A Fabulous Feast

A basket of food is a basket of life.
—*Lozi proverb*

The menu for a grand celebration such as a baby naming ceremony calls for a feast. Depending on your resources, you may want to ask your guests to bring an African dish as part of their contribution to the celebration. Women in Ghana often bring calabash containers of ceremonial sour milk, sweet *munko* cakes of pounded rice, and honey. Gifts of food are popular gifts in many African countries for a naming ceremony. Consequently, for this event one's best china, flatware, and table linens should be used. There are many Afrocentric glass and chinaware patterns that would be suitable for this occasion. Display a floral centerpiece for each dining table. If possible, ask a florist to design them using African flowers and plants.

In keeping with the African tradition, use African sculptures as centerpieces for the dinner table.

The Sacrificial Goat

It is an African tradition to celebrate the baby's name by slaughtering a goat right after the name is given to the baby by the officiant. If it was a wealthy family, the father would slaughter his best cow or sheep. Portions of the meat would be wrapped up and given away to family members to take home for future consumption. The remainder of the meat would be cooked right away as a dish to serve the guests attending the naming ceremony.

The menu for a naming ceremony is more formal than for a baby shower. Some of the popular dishes in African countries are recipes that include goat, beef, olives, yams, plantains, okra, millet (a grain like rice), cassava (similar to a potato), peanuts, coconuts, rice, and fish. Here is a sample of some traditional African and African-American recipes that you may use for your own ceremony.

The sacrificial goat

✳ ✳ ✳ ✳ ✳ ✳ ✳ ✳

Naming Ceremony Menu

Hors d'Oeuvres

Mealy Cornbread
Sweet Potato Pie
Kola Nuts

First Course

Stewed Okra and Tomatoes

Main Course

Senegalese Yassa Chicken
Tunisian Vegetable Cous-Cous

Beverages

Bissap Juice
Senegalese Tea

Dessert

Fresh Fruit

✳ ✳ ✳ ✳ ✳ ✳ ✳ ✳

AFRICAN RECIPES

Senegalese Yassa Chicken

5 large onions, thinly sliced
½ cup fresh lemon juice
⅓ teaspoon salt
¼ teaspoon pepper

¼ teaspoon hot chili pepper
1 cup peanut oil
6 pounds chickens parts (about 2 whole chickens cut up)
1 cup pimiento-stuffed olives

8 carrots, scraped and sliced thin

2 tablespoons Dijon-style mustard

Salt

ground black pepper

⅓ teaspoon chili pepper

In a large mixing bowl, prepare marinade by combining the onion, lemon juice, salt, pepper, ⅛ teaspoon chili pepper, and ¼ cup peanut oil. Place the chicken pieces in the marinade, make sure they are all well covered, and allow them to marinate for 2 hours or more in the refrigerator.

Preheat the broiler to 350 degrees. Take the chicken pieces out of the pan, but save the marinade. Broil in a shallow roasting pan until lightly browned on both sides. Remove the onions only from the marinade. Cook them slowly in 1 tablespoon of peanut oil in a casserole until tender. Add the marinade and heat to a simmer.

Add the broiled chicken pieces to the marinade along with the chili pepper, olives, carrots, mustard, and one cup of water. Mix well, then bring to a boil. Simmer for about 25 minutes or until done. Serve with rice.

SERVES 12

A Healthy Hearth

Homemade cooking from any country can be full of saturated fats, salt, and sugar. Here are a few tips you can use with any recipe to keep your new family healthy:

- Clean away the skin and fat from chicken before cooking it.
- Use low-fat dairy products in recipes.
- Use less than one tablespoon of vegetable oil rather than one tablespoon of butter for marinades and sautés.
- Substitute salt by using lemon juice, garlic, dried herbs, and seasonings.
- Substitute sugar by using natural honey, fruit jams and juice, maple syrup, or molasses.

Tunisian Vegetable Cous-Cous

2 onions, coarsely chopped

2 zucchini or yellow squash, chopped

4 roasted and peeled red bell peppers, sliced

1 cup sliced fresh mushrooms

4 cups chicken broth

4 cups instant cous-cous

4 small tomatoes, coarsely chopped

6 tablespoons vinegar

2 (16-ounce) cans chick peas, drained

2 tablespoons vegetable oil

Sauté the onions and zucchini in oil over a medium flame until tender. Stir in the peppers and mushrooms. Sauté until all vegetables are cooked but still firm. Heat the chicken broth in a saucepan until boiling. Remove from heat and stir in the cous-cous. Let the mixture sit 5 to 7 minutes, then fluff with fork.

In a large bowl, toss the cous-cous with the tomatoes, chickpeas, and vinegar. Stir in the vegetables and their juices. Salt and pepper to taste. Serve at room temperature.

SERVES 12

Kola Nuts

Kola nuts grow on trees. They often have two to six cloves or sides. They are ripe and most often used when they have four cloves on them. The kola nut tastes bitter. These nuts are often crushed to produce the juice used in cola drinks. During traditional African naming ceremonies, each guest is given a whole kola nut to taste and to take home. In Nigeria, to give a kola nut is a sign of friendship.

Gesture of Gratitude

It is an African tradition that during the feast each of the guests should touch the calabash's brim with his or her right hand as a gesture of respect.

Bissap

Bissap is a juice made from the red leaves of the bissap tree in Africa. The leaves are picked and left outside to dry. They are then gathered and boiled. The broth is strained, sweetened, and chilled for consumption. This natural juice tastes like a fruit punch drink. Bissap juice should be available ready-made at any African market or substitute any fruit punch drink.

Senegalese Tea

Though Senegalese tea or green tea is imported from China to Senegal, it is unique because it is served three times to symbolize life stages: the first tea is not sweetened, which symbolizes the pain of childbirth; the second tea is very sweet, which symbolizes the innocence of childhood; the third tea is very strong, so it is bitter, and it symbolizes the hardships of adult life. Tea is also used as a healing drink in many countries, including Africa.

AFRICAN-AMERICAN COUSINS

For a soul food treat, add a sweet potato pie to the menu. Yams were originally brought over from Africa; therefore, sweet potato pie is just a distant kin. Okra also made the journey to America with the first African slaves. Okra was a staple in Africa, where its sap was used to thicken many kinds of stews and was adapted into many kinds of Southern dishes. Also serve cornbread as a side dish. Cornbread is very similar to the "mealy bread" served in various regions in Africa.

Sweet Potato Pie

2 pounds sweet potatoes (about 3 or 4 large)	*½ teaspoon salt*
¼ cup butter, softened	*½ teaspoon nutmeg*
2 cups sugar	*¼ teaspoon ground cloves*
4 eggs	*Can of evaporated milk*
1 teaspoon cinnamon	*9-inch frozen pie crust*

Preheat oven and cookie sheet to 375 degrees. Cook sweet potatoes in boiling water until fork can easily pierce potatoes. Let potatoes cool slightly, then peel. Place peeled potatoes in a large mixing bowl. Beat with an electric mixer until smooth. Stir in butter and sugar. Beat in eggs, one at a time. Mix in spices and evaporated milk. Pour into an unbaked pie crust. Bake on preheated cookie sheet in center of the oven for about 70 minutes or until a knife inserted into the center comes out clean. Cool on wire rack.

SERVES 8 TO 10

Stewed Okra and Tomatoes

1 teaspoon margarine or vegetable oil	*1 can (14½ ounces) no-salt-added whole tomatoes, ½*
½ cup chopped green bell pepper	*drained and chopped*
¼ cup chopped onion	*⅛ teaspoon salt*
1 ten-ounce package frozen cut okra	*½ teaspoon pepper*

Heat the oil in a large saucepan over medium heat. Add the bell pepper and onion, and sauté 3 minutes or until tender. Add the okra, tomatoes, salt, and pepper. Lower heat and simmer, for about 15 to 20 minutes, until okra is tender.

MAKES SIX 1/2-CUP SERVINGS

Mealy Cornbread

1½ cups cornmeal

½ cup all-purpose flour (bleached)

4 teaspoons baking powder

½ teaspoon salt

¼ cup sugar

1 cup whole milk

1 egg, beaten

¼ cup melted butter

In a mixing bowl, combine cornmeal, flour, baking powder, salt, and sugar. In a separate bowl, mix together milk, egg, and butter. Add the liquid mixture to the dry mixture. Stir until the large lumps are removed. Fill greased baking pan or skillet by half. Bake at 425 degrees about 25 minutes or until lightly browned.

MAKES 6 SERVINGS

African Naming Ceremonies

When you follow in the path of your father,
you learn to walk like him.
—*Ashanti proverb*

*N*aming ceremony rituals vary from one African country to the next. Even though there are some differences between countries, the principle remains the same—to give the newborn a meaningful name to carry the baby throughout his or her life.

SOMALIA

When a child is born in Somalia, the new mother and baby stay indoors at home for forty days, a time period known as *afatanbah.* Female relatives and friends visit the family and help take care of them. This includes preparing special foods, such as soup, porridge, and special teas. During the *afatanbah,* the mother wears earrings made from string pulled through a clove of garlic, and the baby wears a bracelet made from string called an *agris gris.* The *agris gris* and garlic are charms that are supposed to ward off those who wish the child harm.

Incense of myrrh is burned twice a day in order to protect the baby from the ordinary smells of the world, which are believed to have the potential to make the child sick.

At the end of the forty days, there is celebration at the home of a friend or relative. This marks the first time the Somalian mother or baby has left the home since the delivery. The naming ceremony then begins. In some families, the naming ceremony occurs within the first two or three weeks of the baby's life. In other families, it is held at the same time as the celebration that is held at the end of the *afatanbah*. These ceremonies are big family gatherings with lots of dancing, singing, music, and food. They also feature prayers and the ritual killing of a goat.

NIGERIA

According to Daffo-Batura custom, when a woman gives birth to her first child, she must remain in her husband's house until the seventh day after the baby is born. Then a naming ceremony takes place. Afterward, the woman and child are taken to the home of the maternal grandparents, where they will remain for two years. This is done as a means of birth control.

KHASI

Among the Khasi, children are named within a day of their birth. The ceremony begins when a relative of the child prepares a sacrifice by pouring rice meal into small dishes and filling a gourd with rice liquor. After an invocation, the relative pours the liquor drop by drop into the rice meal while reciting a list of names. The name the child will have is the one the relative recites during the pouring of the drop of liquor that takes the longest to leave the bottle.

Once the name is found in this way, they anoint the baby's feet with the meal and liquor paste, and the parents and relatives taste the paste. Then, after passing the paste over the baby three times, the father leaves the group to bury the placenta and umbilical cord from the birth the preceding day.

NIGER

Among the Niger and many African societies, the baby is purposely scarred during the naming ceremony in the distinctive patterns of his tribe. At just eight days old, he is given the identifying marks he will carry all of his life. These scars and designs are considered marks of beauty.

IBO

At a baby naming ceremony among the Ibo, the paternal grandparents preside and officiate. The items used in the ceremony include a white cock, four kola nuts, and a yam, which are presented to the priest. The priest in return gives the grandparent cowry shells as payment. The priest is left alone to prepare a feast from the gifts.

After eating the items, the name of the child will come to the priest spiritually. It is believed that if the priest does not perform this rite, good things will not happen in the newborn's life. The naming ceremony is then held on market day (the day everyone goes to the market).

The paternal grandmother prepares two dishes and carries them to her son's house. After the usual breaking of kola nuts and prayers, the food is eaten. The infant's name is then announced. The family and friends dance and sing together until early the following morning.

WOLOF

The Wolof people usually plan a naming ceremony one week after the child is born. There is often a very large gathering of friends and relatives for the rite and celebration. The ceremony is held in the place where the child was born, and it generally begins just before the stroke of noon. On this day, the mother will symbolically sweep out the house, extinguish the fire, and wash the infant in medicinal water. These ritual acts represent the end of one of life's stages and the beginning of another.

Wolof guests bring fine gifts; the men give gifts to the father, the women to the mother. In the center of the compound, a blanket or mat is laid out. On it sits the midwife or a grandmother, holding the infant. The child's head is then shaved, starting on the right side and working to the left, which bestows additional blessings.

Cotton, millet, and red and white kola nuts are gathered in a clay bowl. Red kola nuts symbolize long life, as do white kola nuts. An elder or celebrant will then rub hands all over the infant's head. The celebrant offers a prayer and spits in the child's ear to implant the name in the infant's head. The name is then loudly announced to the gathering, and prayers and libations are offered for health, prosperity, and longevity.

If it is a firstborn child, mother and infant are spirited away and hidden, lest someone should put an "evil eye" on them. A sheep or goat is sacrificed, and the guests spend the rest of the day feasting, singing, and dancing.

thirteen

Naming Ceremonies for Older Folks

No matter how full the river, it still wants to grow.
—*Zairean proverb*

All over the United States, African-American adults are changing their American birth names to African names. After not having control over our families' names during centuries of enslavement, African-Americans are reclaiming the meaningful practice of naming our children. Exercising our hard-earned freedom and rights, we now can even rename ourselves while reclaiming our African origins. The man born Malcolm Little changed his name to the Muslim symbol of "X," to represent the stolen legacy of his unknown family name, and was thereby known as the Minister Malcolm X. This name change was a milestone in Malcolm's life. It was like a rite of passage for his new ministry.

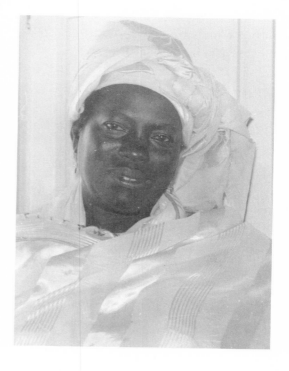

In some African nations, Africans are given new names at various stages of life. For instance, once a child becomes school age, he or she may receive a new name. When a mother has a baby for the first time, she gets a new title. These transition periods are celebrated stages in life's journey and mark the first steps to becoming an adult. Many rites of passage are marked with this type of naming ceremony.

Changing your name in adulthood is not modernistic or extraordinary. It has been well noted in the Bible that several biblical figures' names were changed before they went on to do God's work. Saul, the tax collector's name, was changed to Paul as he was converted. Jacob's name was changed to Israel, which means "Soldier of God." Sarai's name was changed to Sarah, and Abram's name was changed to Abraham before God made them the mother and father of nations. For many folks, religious or not, changing names during adulthood is often a catalyst for change.

African-American adults are increasingly participating in adult versions of this rite of passage. More and more adults are changing or adding new names to their existing names. Many are also changing their children's names. Some famous African-Americans who have changed their American birth names to meaningful African names over the years include:

AMERICAN BIRTH NAME/AFRICAN NAME	WHO ARE THEY?
Cassius Clay/Muhammad Ali	heavyweight boxing champion
Stokely Carmichael/Kwame Toure	civil rights leader
Lew Alcindor/Kareem Abdul-Jabbar	NBA Hall of Famer
Arthur Lee Smith Jr./Molefi Kete Asante	father of Afrocentricity
Frizzell Gray/Kweisi Mfume	president of the NAACP
LeRoi Jones/Amiri Baraka	poet-playwright
Ron Everett/Maulana Karenga	Kwanzaa founder
Don L. Lee/Haki Madhubuti	poet
H. Rap Brown/Jamil Abdullah Al-Amin	civil rights leader

Kweisi Mfume (pronounced "Kwah-ee-see Oom-Foo-May"), the president of the National Association for the Advancement of Colored People (NAACP), changed his American name. His original birth name was Frizzell Gray. The name Kweisi Mfume is Swahili for "Conquering son of kings." His great-aunt brought back a befitting indigenous name from the coast of West Africa especially for him. She told him that "the vibrations in the name will help you to be what you must be. Always be true to yourself and your name will carry you. But if you bring dishonor to your new name, it will forsake you. You are Kweisi now . . . Kweisi Mfume."

Molefi Kete Asante (pronounced "Moe-lef-ee Kee-tay Aa-san-tay") is the African name of an author and the head of Temple University's African-American Studies Department. His birth name was Arthur Lee Smith Jr. He states, "I changed my name for three main reasons: for history—to become more historically correct; for psychology—to deal with my mind as an African-American man; and for culture—to demonstrate pride in my own cultural background."

THE POSSIBILITIES

Naming ceremonies for older folks can be just as elaborate as a baby naming ceremony can be. If you would like to make a change, go for it. Pull out all the stops. Believe in yourself. You are worth it and why not have a name that proves it? You can combine the naming ceremony with a rite-of-passage program or a birthday celebration. It's your day. This is a time of renewal and rejuvenation. You should feel that before you were just a gray cocoon and inside you now is a person who is experiencing a metamorphosis. Soon you will become a beautiful black butterfly with strong wings and the ability to fly as high as you want.

THE ADULT NAMING CEREMONY

A Midlife Crisis

My fiftieth birthday was soon approaching. A few of my friends, who were also turning fifty, and I decided to hold a rite of passage, which included a naming ceremony for ourselves. We had African *mameboyes* [matching fabric for a headwrap and dress] designed for the occasion, and we secretly picked out our names beforehand. We also ordered gold Egyptian charms and necklaces with our new African names inscribed in hieroglyphics on them for the occasion. Each of us had a close family member put our necklaces around our necks, which made our new names official.

—Sierra, Oakland, California

A naming ceremony for an adult is different from that for an infant because of the history associated with living under the old name. The recommended steps for an adult naming ceremony follow:

Opening the ceremony · The ritual begins with a libation that asks for God's blessing while inviting our African ancestors to join the ceremony from the East, West, North, and South.

Acknowledging the old · Choose something you want to change in your present life and sets a goal for the future. Your choices are written on paper and placed in a fireproof urn or metal container.

Casting off the old · Burn the paper in the urn.

Your story · A storyteller may be hired to tell a story of rebirth, or a family member can be assigned a poem to read or a story to tell.

Acknowledging the new · The new name of your choice is announced to all of your guests. Describe how your name was chosen and what it means. The ashes from the paper that was burned are then smeared on your forehead. You may want to commemorate the occasion by putting your name on a piece of jewelry at this time. Small gifts are then presented to each of the guests.

Thanksgiving and celebration · Offer a prayer or blessing and then thank all of the family and friends who are there to support you. The gifts from the guests can then be opened, followed by dancing and feasting. At the celebration, it's always nice to play inspirational songs, like "Ain't No Stopping Us Now" by McFadden and Whitehead, and "I Believe" by the Sounds of Blackness.

Appropriate gifts to give your guests include these:

> flowers
> a Christmas ornament that reads "A gift from . . ."
> personalized pens or pencils labeled "A gift from . . ."
> ethnic-print-covered blank book
> baskets
> personalized storybook
> an Afrocentric card with a personal message and an Afrocentric bookmark

Appropriate gifts from guests include these:

> flower bulbs to plant (to symbolize rebirth)
> jewelry
> African-American daily meditation books
> African heritage Bible
> personalized gift (if the guests know the name ahead of time)
> ethnic photo album
> African doll
> African art print
> African sculpture

Legally Changing Your Name

FOR ADULTS

To legally change a name, usually one must hire an attorney. The attorney will file a petition in court to have the name changed. In order to file the petition, the adult will need to have on hand a copy of his or her original birth certificate. Most times the person changing his or her name will not have to appear in court. The judge will decide on whether or not to change a person's name. There are a few reasons why a judge would rule against a name change. For instance, if there is reason to suspect you are changing your name to avoid paying creditors or trying to avoid criminal prosecution.

FOR CHILDREN

Children under two years of age can usually have their birth certificate changed through the state's vital statistics department. For older children, the parents will have to hire an attorney to file a petition in court to have the child's name changed. In order to file a petition, the court will need to secure the permission of both of the parents.

Whether you are naming a new baby, renaming an older child, or even giving yourself a new name, a name change should give your child and you great pride and joy. A name should inspire and encourage you to be the best person you can be. Let the name you choose be a springboard for your greatness that lies ahead.

IV

What a person possesses is not stronger than himself.

—*Nigerian proverb*

ADULT RITES-OF-PASSAGE

African-American Women on Tour
3914 Murphy Canyon Road, Suite 216-B
San Diego, CA 92123
800-560-2298
858-560-2770

Five-city annual conference series, reaching more than four thousand women each year. National touring group with a rites-of-passage program for young girls and women. Focus is on individual healing and community building among Black women.

AFRICAN ATTIRE FOR ADULTS

4 W Circle
704 Fulton Street
Brooklyn, NY 11238
718-875-6500

Creates African-centered men's and women's wear.

M&M Sport Specialties
2122 South Chickasaw Trail, Suite 120
Orlando, FL 32825
407-380-5406

Unique batik clothing.

Pan-African Connection
300 Beckley Avenue
Dallas, TX 75203
214-943-8262

Contemporary wear made from African fabric for women and men.

Therez Fleetwood
New York, NY 10001
212-714-8058

Elegant fashion, home decor, children's items, accessories, gifts, jewelry, toys, stationery, and bridal wear.

AFRICAN ATTIRE FOR CHILDREN

Jason & Jourdon, Ltd.
2900 Largo Road
Upper Marlboro, MD 20772
301-627-1966

Afrocentric children's wear.

Moshood NY
698 Fulton Street
Brooklyn, NY 11217
718-243-9433
718-243-2451 fax

An Afrocentric clothing designer. Call for a catalog.

Moshood Atlanta
217 Mitchell Street
Atlanta, GA 30303
404-523-9433
404-523-9430 fax

An Afrocentric clothing designer. Call for a catalog.

BABY REGISTRIES

Babies "R" Us (Toys "R" Us)
888-BABYRUS

Let your friends and family purchase exactly what you need for your baby. Choose the gifts you want using their state-of-the-art hand-held scanner. Get free shower invitations and a five-dollar coupon.

Service Merchandise
800-251-1212

Call for a kit and free announcement cards.

Target
800-800-8800

Scan the gift items you want.

USA Baby
800-323-4108
800-996-BABY (IL)

Shower gift registry.

BALLOONS

Pioneer Balloon Network
800-803-5591
www.qualtex.com

Nationwide network of professional balloon artists who will create giant towers, sculptures, and balloon drops for any occasion.

CAKE DESIGNERS

Chris' Cakes
2812 West Florence Avenue
Los Angeles, CA 90043
213-750-7320
213-750-2640 fax

Specializes in cakes for baby showers.

Isn't That Special—Outrageous Cakes
720 Monroe Street
Hoboken, NJ 07030
201-216-0123

Cultural and special-occasion cakes.

CATERERS

Dee Dee Dailey
Brooklyn, NY 11238
718-615-1654

By appointment only. Continental and vegetarian cuisine.

The Elegant Difference
Cleveland, OH 44120
216-751-4143

By appointment only. Specializes in Southern cuisine.

Obaa Koryoe Restaurant and Cafe
3143 Broadway
New York, New York 10027
212-316-2950

Specializes in West African cuisine.

DRUMMERS, DANCERS, AND
STILT-WALKERS

Djoniba Dance & Drum Centre
37 18th Street 7th floor
New York, NY 10003
212-477-3464
212-254-9466 fax
info@djoniba.com

*This is a resource for dancers, musicians, fire
eaters, masks, and acrobatic stilt-walkers.*

Khalidah's North Afrikan Dance Experience
5306 South Cornell Avenue
Chicago, IL 60615
773-324-9305
773-955-9305 fax
info@khalidahsdance.twoffice.com

*Fine adaptations and renditions of dance
techniques indigenous to North Africa. This
company provides dancers who specialize in
North African dance.*

Dimensions Dance Theater
Alice Arts Center
1428 Alice Street, 3rd floor
Oakland, CA 94612-4004

510-465-3363
510-465-3364 fax
dimensionsdance@prodigy.net

*Various programs of African dance
and storytelling.*

African Caribbean Dance Theatre, Inc.
P.O. Box 10943
Tallahassee, FL 32302
850-539-4087
acdt93@aol.com

*Nonprofit performing-arts organization
providing an exchange for African and
Caribbean dance styles.*

FLORISTS

Bloomers, Ltd.
1216 North Charles Street
Baltimore, MD 21201
410-752-8850

Domestic and exotic floral arrangements.

Daily Blossom
236 West 27th Street
New York, NY 10001
212-633-9000
212-554-4600

*African-American owned florist who
provides a variety of generally available
flower arrangements.*

Mitchell's Florist
501 Fairvilla Road
Orlando, FL 32808
407-298-0703

*By appointment only. Offers floral
arrangements that can be customized with
requested African flowers and plants. Also
African-American owned and operated.*

Terry's Enchanted Garden
19338 Livernois
Detroit, MI 48221
313-342-3758

*This African-American owned and operated
company offers unique flower arrangements
for a variety of events and celebrations.*

GIFTS

African Aerobic Videos
Ave Montague
One Hallidie Plaza, Suite 701
San Francisco, CA 94102
415-346-1183

Featuring African dance.

The African-American Museum Shop
3536 Grand Avenue
Dallas, TX 75210
214-565-9026

Offers unique African-American gifts.

Afrocentric City
Cheltenham Square Mall
2385 Cheltenham Avenue
Philadelphia, PA 19119
215-887-2559

*A large selection of African sculptures,
artifacts, fabric, and gifts for purchase.*

Artful Greetings
800-638-2733
www.artfulgreetings.com

*Beautiful framed and double-matted
mini-prints of African-American children.*

Avon Centre Spa, Salon and Store
Trump Tower
725 Fifth Avenue
New York, NY 10022
888-577-2866 (salon)
800-367-2866, ext. 1 (mail order)

African-American gifts. Call for a free catalog.

Black Images Book Bazaar
230 Wynnewood Village
Dallas, TX 75241
214-943-0142
800-272-5027

Gifts, herbs, and oils.

Charlotte's Ceramics
Warrensville Heights, OH 44320
216-663-3273

By appointment only. African-American ceramic birth plates, Black porcelain, dolls and gifts.

Craft Caravan
63 Green Street
New York, NY 10012
212-431-6669

Imported African handicrafts and jewelry.

Essence Essentials
1500 Broadway
New York, NY 10036
800-6-ESSENCE (mail order)

African-inspired gift collection and attire. Call for free catalog.

The Gold Connection
9146 West Florist
St. Louis, MO 63136
314-867-7400
www.goldconnection.com

Specializing in Kemetic and Adinkra symbols in jewelry.

From the Heart of Africa
120 North 63rd Street
Philadelphia, PA 19139
215-471-5119

Imported African gifts, including Black angels, calabash bowls, and Kenyan sandstone eggs.

House of Oasala
235 Washington Avenue
Brooklyn, NY 11205
718-638-2871

Imported Nigerian handicrafts and musical instruments.

International Star Registry
34523 Wilson Road
Ingleside, IL 60041
800-282-3333
847-546-5533

Officially name an actual star. A framed certificate will be shipped to you with all the information about your star.

J C Penney's Influences
Department 100
Atlanta, GA 30390
800-222-6161 (mail order)

African-inspired gift collection and attire. Call for free catalog.

Kuumba Place
EE Hale House
12 Morley Street
Roxbury, MA 02119
617-427-8325

Quilts, wall hangings, and tapestries made from traditional fabrics.

My Day
P.O. Box 55152
Atlanta, GA 30308
770-736-3508

Poster of your child's name and family history with African textile patterns. Framed and unframed available.

National Museum of African Art Gift Shop
950 Independence Avenue
Washington, DC 20560
202-786-2147

Offers unique African gifts.

Rhythm & Hues Quilts
New Orleans, Lane
504-944-7984, ext. 4

African-American handmade quilts with ethnic scenes.

Russ Berrie and Company
111 Bauer Drive
Oakland, NJ 07436
201-337-9000

"I Am the Big Sister/Brother" buttons.

Spiegels E-Style
800-SPIEGEL

African and African-inspired gift collection and attire. Call for a free catalog.

Studio Museum of Harlem Gift Shop
144 West 125th Street
New York, NY 10027
212-864-4500, ext. 237

Afrocentric gifts. Free catalog.

Sweet Plum Collections
P.O. Box 130339
Laurelton, NY 11413
800-272-5160

Beautiful brown faces on a bed linen for little girls. Call for a brochure.

INVITATIONS, THANK-YOU CARDS, AND DECORATIONS

Africonia, Inc.
11554 East 169th Street
Artesia, CA 90701
703-631-7713
310-402-2364

"Baby blessings" Afrocentric shower gift bags.

American Greeting Company
One American Road
Cleveland, OH 44144
216-252-7300

Kente-patterned paper plates, cups, and napkins.

The Beistle Company
P.O. Box 10
Shippensburg, PA 17257
717-532-2135
800-445-2131 (fax order)

African-American baby cutout decorations.

Black Butterfly Greeting Cards
P.O. Box 21521
El Sobrante, CA 94820
603-297-2129 (fax order)
www.blackbutterflycards.com

*Offers Afrocentric cards for all occasions.
Series of African-American baby shower cards.*

Carole Joy Creations
107 Mill Plain Road, Suite 200
Danbury, CT 16811
203-798-2060

*African-American baby shower cards and
invitations.*

Color of the World
186-A Skokie Valley Road
Highland Park, IL 60035
847-831-2762
www.gianna@colorworld.com

*African-American baby shower invitations
and baby clothes.*

Create-a-Camera
1040 West 2nd Street
Pomona, CA 91766
www.bestcamera.com
bestcamera@aol.com
888-BEST-CAM (800-410-8008)

*Provides disposable embossed cameras with
the parents' or baby's name. Price includes
developing and complimentary table cards
for each guest.*

Frederick Douglass Designs
1033 Folger Street
Berkeley, CA 94710
800-399-4430
510-204-0950
www.fddesigns.com

*African-American baby shower cards.
Call for catalog.*

Hallmark Mahogany
2501 McGee Street
Kansas City, MO 64108
800-650-4505

*Offers more than 900 cultural cards for almost
every season, including the Iyanla Vanzant
collection.*

Heart Thoughts
6200 East Central, Suite 100
Wichita, KS 67208-4282
800-524-2229

*African-American baby shower invitations
and announcements with custom imprinting.
Call for a catalog.*

Jade Ethnic Cards and Gifts
P.O. Box 78115
Seattle, WA 98178
800-866-4880
206-725-3445

OFFICIANTS

Iyalosha Ade Kola Adedapo
Milwaukee, WI 53208
414-483-9892

*By appointment only. Yoruba Shango
priestess performs traditional ceremonies
and storytelling.*

Oyafunmike Ogunlano
New York area
212-802-7114

*By appointment only. She performs naming
ceremonies and storytelling.*

Starspirits
Philadelphia and the Tri-State area
800-583-9963
215-763-4054

Spiritual naming and ceremonies.

STORYTELLERS

Akbar Imhotep
P.O. Box 11386
Atlanta, GA 30310
404-688-3376

Storyteller, puppeteer, and puppetmaker.

Donna Washington
P.O. Box 1323
Evanston, IL 60204
708-475-8051

*Multicultural folklorist and storyteller; will
custom design folktales for your event.*

Kala Jojo
c/o Keepers of the Culture
P.O. Box 15083
Philadelphia, PA 19130
215-849-4254
800-920-9627

This tall-story teller for hire plays authentic African instruments and sings. Cassette tapes available.

Mama Edie
The Chicago Association of Black
Storytellers
c/o Fox Valley Folklore Society
755 North Evanslawn Avenue
Aurora, IL 60506
312-768-6773

Folk storyteller and singer.

Shanta
c/o Artist of Note
P.O. Box 11
Kaneville, IL 60144
800-249-0863
312-994-5554

Traditional African and spiritual storytelling and music.

Appendix A

AFROCENTRIC PATTERNS FOR INVITATIONS, DECORATIONS, AND PARTY FAVORS

Kuba Cloth

East African Print

Ghana Mudcloth Print

Adinkra Print

Fertility Dolls

African-American Contemporary

Appendix B

POPULAR URBAN NAMES

Girls

A
Aallayah
Aallleighya
Aalming
Aamy
Abriana
Abrianna
Achara
Adalia
Adela
Adelaide
Adia
Adicia
Adina
Adine
Adria
Adrian
Adrienne
Afeni
Afre
Africa
Afyia
Aiesha
A'isha
Akeia
Akeiyla

Akiba
Akila
Akilah
Akira
Akiriya
Akiya
Alana
Alcola
Aleale
Alescia
Alexis
Alfre
Allar
Allen
Alliya
Alresa
Altonette
Amarika
Amaryia
Amaryllis
Amber
Amethia
Amira
Amitra
Anareal
Andrion
Aneas
Aneesa

Aneesha
Aneisha
Angelique
Anisha
Anitra
Annae
Antonia
Antonya
Aretha
Arlethia
Arnel
Arthel
Artise
Asion
A'tasha
A-tle
Atiya
Atoya
Aurelia
Autumn
Avriann
Ayana
Ayanna
Azia

B
Baileen
Banetta

149

Begona
Bequell
Bernetha
Bertena
Bertrise
Bianca
Bianna
Brana
Brandy
Bre'anna
Bre'anne
Bre'ara
Bre-Ann
Bre-Anna
Brea
Breah
Breana
Breanda
Breann
Breanna
Breannah
Breanne
Breanya
Breaona
Brear
Breauna
Breaunne
Breawn
Breawna
Breay
Bree
Breea
Breeahna
Breean
Breeana
Breeann
Breeanna

Breeanne
Breeauna
Breelyn
Breeon
Brei
Breia
Breiana
Breiann
Breianna
Breigh
Breighann
Breijanna
Breila
Breion
Brenda
Brendella
Breona
Breonia
Breonna
Breyanna
Breyona
Bria
Briah
Briahna
Briana
Brianda
Briane
Briann
Brianna
Briannah
Brianne
Brianni
Briannon
Briauna
Brie-Ann
Brie-Anne
Brie

Brieann
Brieanna
Brieannah
Brieanne
Brielle
Briena
Brienna
Brienne
Brieon
Briet
Brieta
Brietta
Briette
Brigetta
Brndell
Briona
Brione
Brionna
Brionne
Brita
Britny
Brucetta
Bruchetta
Brya
Bryah
Bryana
Bryann
Bryanna
Bryanne
Bryawna
Butterfly

C
Caiya
Calista
Cambria
Camille

Candice

Candience

Candis

Cantrice

Carsandra

Carsietta

Caryne

Casanara

Cashana

Cassandra

Catrina

Ceharra

Ceira

Celecia

Ceseli

Chaille

Chalissa

Chalon

Chalonn

Chalonna

Chalonne

Chanda

Chandra

Chanel

Chanise

Chanrice

Chantae

Chantai

Chantarai

Chantay

Chantaye

Chante

Chantea

Chanteau

Chantee

Chanteese

Chantel

Chanter

Chantess

Chantey

Chantez

Chanti

Chantoya

Chantrea

Chantrel

Chantrell

Chantrelle

Chantrille

Chanty

Chaprella

Charelle

Charkeita

Charla

Charleetah

Charlita

Charlotte

Charmaine

Charnita

Chatrelle

Chauntay

Chaunte

Chauntea

Chauntee

Chelayane

Chellise

Chemier

Cherly

Chevelle

Chevonne

Chinelle

Chissanna

Chitquita

Choclate

Cian

Ciana

Cianna

Cieairria

Ciehra

Ciera

Cierah

Cierra

Cissy

Cita

Cladrena

Cleona

Clister

Colene

Conita

Constance

Coretta

Corine

Corlisa

Corlise

Corliss

Corlissa

Corly

Countice

Cozetta

Crystal

Curtesa

Curtina

Cyana

Cyerra

Cyiarra

Cynthia

D

Daedra

Daejah

Daejanae

Daesha

Daeshan
Daeshanda
Daeshandra
Daeshandria
Daeshaun
Daeshauna
Daeshaundra
Daeshaundria
Daeshavon
Daeshawn
Daeshawna
Daeshawnda
Daeshawndra
Daeshawndria
Daeshawntia
Daeshon
Daeshona
Daeshonda
Daija
Daisha
Daisia
Daja
DaJona
Dakota
Dallison
Daloris
Damara
Damari
Damariae
Dana
Daneca
Daneka
Danielle
Danyelle
Dannette
Dara
Daressa

Darla
Dasha
Dashawn
Dashawna
Dashawnda
Dashay
Dashell
Dashevona
Dashonda
Dasia
Dason
Davanta
Davante
Davina
Davonte
Davontia
Day'sha
Daymaria
Dayon
Daystina
De'Anna
De'Borah
De'Celle
De'Lawn
De'Lisha
De'Lores
De'marion
De'Nossis
De'shon
De'shonda
De'Wanda
Debara
Deda
Dedra
Deicy
Deisha
Dejaneira

Dejanelle
Dejanna
Dejean
Dejhane
Dejia
Dejoria
Dejounae
Dejovaline
Dejuna
Delacia
Delilah
Delplesa
Demaree
Demari
Demaria
Demarri
Demetress
Demetria
Demetricia
DeMonet
Dené
Denishia
Denyce
Deronda
Desaire
Desana
Deshae
Deshan
Deshanda
Deshandra
Deshane
Deshaun
Deshaundra
Deshawn
Deshawna
Deshawndra
Deshaya

Desheania
Deshona
Deshonda
Deshonna
Deshunta
Desiree
Desreta
Desria
Destiny
Devisha
Devon
Devonna
Devontea
Devony
Diaja
Dionisia
Divan
Djana
Dolitha
Dollecia
Dominique
Donna
Donnelle
Donta
Dontrelle
Doreen
Dorsey
Duchess
Dyshanta
Dyshawn
Dyshawna
Dyshonda
Dyshonna

E
Earlene
Earline

Ebenita
Ebonie
Ebony
Eddimae
Edesa
Edwina
Eleacia
Eleasha
Elecia
Eleesha
Eleisha
Elesha
Eleshia
Eleticia
Elicia
Elida
Elidia
Eliscia
Elisha
Elishia
Elishua
Eliska
Elita
Elitia
Elitie
Ellecia
Ellesha
Ellexia
Ellisha
Ellita
Ellitia
Ellitie
Elois
Elsha
Elshunta
Elvinie
Elysha

Erykah
Essence
Eania

F
Fai
Fajah
Fawn
Fawnette
Felnicia
Fornesha
Francelle
Frances
Fredimae

G
Gelisa
Georgiann
Gerree
Gerren
Gillisa
Ginetta
Gladys
Gracilyn
Gwendolyn

H
Hazel
Henrietta
Herbertia
Hosanna
Hudain
Hyacinth

I
Illisha
Ilysia

Imelda	Janiya	Jowan
Isha	Jaqyrah	Julene
Ivory	Jarica	Juwana
	Jarika	
J	Jasmine	K
J'vonne	Jatana	Kaandra
J'vonté	Jatara	Kadisha
Ja'net	Jataria	Kaeha
Ja-Cheyla	Jatarra	Kaeona
Ja-elle	Javana	Kaha
Ja-Leesa	Javeera	Kahneisha
Ja-Lisa	Javina	Kaia
Ja-Vonya	Javon	Kaiha
Jabria	Javonda	Kaiya
Jabriona	Javone	Kaja
Jacinta	Javonna	Kala
Jack-ee	Javonne	Kalahn
Jacquie	Javonya	Kalan
Jai'breon	Jawana	Kaleena
Jai'lysa	Jawanna	Kaleenda
Jai-Vonna	Jawn	Kaleesha
Jaleasa	Jaybrié	Kalen
Jaleesa	Jaylanae	Kalena
Jaleisa	Jazmine	Kalese
Jalesa	Jelan	Kalilia
Jalicia	Jelisa	Kalimah
Jalisa	Jenae	Kalin
Jalise	Jenera	Kalina
Jalissa	Jenesia	Kalinda
Jalizé	Jillisa	Kalindi
Jamesetta	Joanne	Kalinna
Jamila	Jocelyn	Kalisa
Jamira	Joelle	Kalise
Janaera	Jolice	Kalisha
Janaisia	Jonetta	Kalissa
Janena	Jordynn	Kallan
Janilla	Jovita	Kallen

Kallin
Kallon
Kallyn
Kalon
Kalyn
Kalynda
Kalysa
Kalyssa
Kameshia
Kaneasha
Kaneesha
Kaneisha
Kanesha
Kaneshia
Kaniesha
Kanisha
Kanishia
Kanita
Kara
Karea
Kareen
Karenca
Karlene
Karnecha
Karysha
Kashawn
Kasmira
Kassandra
Kaya
Kayana
Kayanne
Kea
Keana
Keandra
Keani
Keanna
Keayra

Keena
Keenya
Kehana
Keiana
Keianna
Keina
Keionna
Keisha
Keishae
Keishaun
Keishauna
Keishawn
Keishianna
Keja
Kendea
Kendra
Kendria
Kenneisha
Kenya
Kenyada
Keona
Keoni
Keonna
Keshanna
Keshila
Keva
Keya
Keyana
Keyannie
Keyauna
Keyna
Keyona
Keyondra
Keyonna
Khadija
Khandi
Khay

Khiana
Khianna
Ki'jana
Kia
Kiae
Kiah
Kiahna
Kiahni
Kiana
Kiandre
Kianha
Kiani
Kianna
Kianni
Kiara
Kiauna
Kiaundra
Kiaya
Kierna
Kierstin
Kimbra
Kimbria
Kimbrie
Kina
Kineesha
Kineisha
Kinesha
Kineshia
Kinisha
Kinishia
Kiona
Kionah
Kioni
Kionia
Kionna
Kionte
Kisha

Kishahna
Kishanda
Kishaun
Kishawn
Kiya
Kiyaan
Kiyana
Kiyanna
Kneshia
Konyali
Kristian
Kwaniesha
Kya
Kyana
Kyanee
Kyann
Kyanna
Kyanua
Kyeisha
Kyla

L
La'Rae
La'Rhonda
La'Shawn
La'Sondra
La'Wanda
La-bon
La-Dale
La-Dawnn
La-Don
La-Donna
La-juan
La-juana
La-Keysha
La-Neece
La-Neesa

La-Neisha
La-Neishah
Lanette
La-rhonda
La-Shauna
La-Shaunda
La-shawn
La-Shonna
La-Shonnah
La-sondra
La-Teesha
La-Ticia
La-Tosha
La-trice
Lachanda
Lachonda
Lacreash
Lacreashia
Lacrecia
Lacresha
Lacreshia
Lacresia
Lacretia
Lacricia
Lacrisha
Lacrishia
Ladawn
Ladawna
Ladesha
Ladonna
Ladonne
Ladonya
Ladricka
Lady
Lajuana
Lajuanna
Lakaiesha

Lakaisha
Lakasha
Lakeesha
Lakeeta
Lakendra
Lakenya
Laniece
Lanise
Lanisha
Laprincess
Laquanna
Laqueen
Laqueinta
Laqueisha
Laquinta
Larah
Larhonda
Lashana
Lashanay
Lashanda
Lashandra
Lashandria
Lashanna
Lashannon
Lashanta
Lashante
Lashauna
Lashaunda
Lashaundra
Lashaunna
Lashawna
Lashawnda
Lashawndra
Lashawnia
Lashona
Lashonda
Lashondia

Lashondra
Lashonna
Latacia
Lataesha
Lataisha
Latana
Latandra
Latania
Latanja
Latanna
Latanya
Latascha
Lataschia
Latasha
Latashia
Lataysha
Latea
Lateasha
Lateashia
Lateasia
Latecia
Lateesha
Latifah
Latisa
Latisha
Latishia
Latissa
Latissha
Latitia
Lativa
Latiya
Latoia
Latoiya
Latona
Latonya
Latoria
Latosha

Latoshia
Latoya
Latoye
Latoyia
Latrece
Latrecia
Latrica
Latrice
Latricia
Latrina
Latrisha
Latrishia
Lavern
Laverna
Laverne
Lavetta
LaVonne
LaWana
Lawanda
Le'kenyada
Le-noria
Le-quisha
Lecea
Lecia
Lee-na
Leecia
Leesha
Leesia
Leia
Lekeesha
Lekenya
Lekesha
Lekeshia
Lekresha
Lela
Lena
Lenece

Leneisha
Lenesha
Lenoria
Leshawna
Leshondra
Leslie
Letasha
Letise
Letreece
Letrice
Lieta
Lovely
Lynda
Lynita

M
Madelyn
Maiya
Makeva
Malene
Marietta
Marisha
Marleen
Marlissa
Marquita
Marta
Martha
Matrice
Mattie
Maya
Meleia
Meleisha
Melia
Meliah
Melida
Melika
Melna

Mercedes
Mia
Miasha
Miaya
Milah
Milia
Milica
Milka
Milla
Minnie
Miranda
Mishon
Miya
Monay
Monette
Mya
Mychele

N
Nassiya
Nadijah
Nakesha
Nancy
Nandi
Nashana
Nashanda
Nashauna
Nashaunda
Nashawn
Nashawna
Nashida
Nashounda
Nashuana
Natalie
Natisha
Necie
Neishia

Neissia
Nickquasha
Nidya
Nikisha
Nikkya
Nisha
Nyda
Nydia

O
Octavia
Oleta
Oletha
Onvia
Opra
Oprah
Orinthia
Ornella
Ouiana
Otesa

P
Patrice
Paulette
Paulina
Precious
Princess

Q
Quanesha
Quanesia
Quaneta
Quaniesha
Queen
Queenie
Quiana
Quyana

R
Rakesha
Rakisha
Ranell
Ranelle
Rashaan
Rashana
Rashanda
Rashani
Rashanta
Rashauna
Rashaundra
Rashawn
Rashawna
Rasheba
Rasheen
Rashida
Rashon
Rashona
Rashonda
Rashunda
Raven
Regime
Regine
Renell
Reshana
Reshaunda
Reshawna
Reshawnda
Reshawnna
Reshonda
Reshonn
Reshonta
Rhoshanda
Riquel
Rochelle
Roma

Rona
Roneeka
Roneice
Roneisha
Ronelle
Roneshia
Roni
Ronia
Ronice
Roshanna
Roshanta
Roshaun
Roshawn
Roshawna
Roshawnda
Roshawnna
Roshona
Roshonda
Roshunda
Rositha
Roslin
Ruby
Rudee

S
Sabrena
Sakeenah
Samara
Santana
Sapphire
Schanel
Schanell
Scherise
Seanna
Searria
Seira
Seirra

Sessillee
ShaDonna
Shakayla
Shakeeyah
Shakeia
Shakiva
Shalese
Shaleta
Shaletta
Shalice
Shalicia
Shalida
Shalila
Shalilah
Shalisa
Shalise
Shalisha
Shalisse
Shalita
Shalitta
Shalona
Shalonda
Shalonde
Shamar
Shan-non
Shanda
Shandah
Shandee
Shandi
Shandice
Shandra
Shandri
Shandria
Shandry
Shanece
Shaneese
Shaneeta

Shaneice
Shaneikah
Shaneisha
Shaneka
Shanekia
Shanell
Shanella
Shanelle
Shanequa
Shanesha
Shaneshia
Shanesia
Shanessa
Shaneta
Shanetha
Shanetta
Shanette
Shaneva
Shaneyka
Shanica
Shanice
Shaniece
Shanieka
Shanika
Shanikah
Shanikia
Shanikka
Shanikqua
Shaniqua
Shanique
Shanise
Shanisha
Shanissha
Shanita
Shanta
Shantee
Shantai

Shantana
Shantay
Shantaya
Shantaye
Shantayna
Shantaynah
Shanté
Shante
Shantea
Shanteca
Shantee
Shanteena
Shanteka
Shantera
Shantese
Shanti
Shantia
Shantice
Shantie
Shantina
Shantise
Shantisha
Shantoya
Shantreece
Shantrell
Shantrese
Shantrice
Shanttoria
Shaquan
Shaquana
Shaquanda
Shaquandra
Shaquanera
Shaquanna
Shaquita
Shara
Shareese

Shareeta
Sharesa
Sharese
Sharette
Sharice
Shariece
Sharis
Sharise
Sharisha
Shariss
Sharisse
Sharita
Sharla
Sharnease
Sharneese
Sharneisha
Sharnese
Sharnise
Sharonda
Sharrita
Shashawn
Shasity
Shatara
Shatoya
Shauna
Shaunda
Shaundra
Shaundrea
Shaundree
Shaundria
Shaundrice
Shaunice
Shaunta
Shauntae
Shauntay
Shaunte
Shauntea

Shauntee
Shauntia
Shauntice
Shauntrell
Shauntrelle
Shavaugn
Shavoan
Shavonne
Shawana
Shawanda
Shawanna
Shawannah
Shawante
Shawna
Shawnda
Shawndah
Shawndra
Shawndrea
Shawndria
Shawnta
Shawntae
Shawntay
Shawnte
Shawntea
Shawntia
Shayla
Sheena
Shekeia
Sheketa
Shekia
Shekiah
Shekita
Sheleza
Shelica
Shelicia
Shelisa
Shelise

Shelisse
Shelita
Sheliza
Shemikah
Shenae
Shenay
Shenda
Shenee
Sheneena
Shenequa
Shenice
Shenika
Shenina
Sheniqua
Shenise
Shenita
Shenna
Shequida
Shequita
Sherece
Sheree
Shereece
Shereen
Shereese
Sherelle
Sheresa
Sherese
Shereta
Sheretta
Sherette
Sherice
Shericia
Sheriece
Sherilyn
Sherise
Sherissa
Sherisse

Sherita
Sherlon
Sherrell
Sherrish
Sherrita
Sherryse
Sheryce
Shikia
Shikita
Shikitha
Shilla
Shimika
Shinnil
Shinetra
Shirlene
Shironda
Shona
Shonda
Shondia
Shondie
Shondra
Shonelle
Shonta
Shontae
Shontai
Shontal
Shontalee
Shontara
Shontasia
Shontavia
Shontaviea
Shontay
Shontaya
Shonte
Shontecia
Shontedra
Shontee

Shontel
Shontelle
Shonteral
Shonteria
Shontessia
Shonti
Shontia
Shontina
Shoreen
Sianni
Siara
Siarah
Siarra
Siarrah
Sieara
Siearra
Siera
Sierah
Sieria
Sierra
Sierrah
Sierre
Simmina
Skylar
Syerr
Sylvia
Syreeta
Syretta

T
Ta-Lisa
Ta-neka
Tacha
Tachell
Tachia
Tachiana
Taesha

Taheisha

Tahisha

Tahneisha

Tahnisha

Tahsha

Taiesha

Taija

Taileisha

Taima

Taisha

Taiwana

Taiwanna

Taja

Tajahnique

Tajanae

Tajuana

Tajuanna

Takara

Takarra

Takeara

Takeisha

Takenia

Takenja

Takenya

Takesha

Takeshia

Takesia

Takira

Takiria

Takisha

Takishea

Takishia

Takita

Takiya

Takra

Takyrah

Talasea

Talasia

Talayna

Taleesha

Taleis

Taleisha

Talena

Talesa

Talesha

Taleshia

Talesia

Talicia

Taliesha

Talina

Talinda

Taline

Talisa

Talisha

Talysha

Tamaka

Tamaki

Tamako

Tamala

Tamarah

Tameca

Tamecia

Tamecka

Tameeka

Tameica

Tameka

Tameke

Tamekia

Tamela

Tamelia

Tamera

Tamesha

Tameshia

Tamica

Tamiecka

Tamieka

Tamika

Tamikah

Tamike

Tamikia

Tamikka

Tamikoa

Tamila

Tamilla

Tamille

Tamillia

Tamilya

Tamiqua

Tamisha

Tamishia

Tamnesha

Tamreeka

Tamrika

Tamura

Tanak

Tanasha

Tanashia

Tanay

Tanda

Tandeka

Tandi

Tandie

Tandis

Tandra

Tandria

Tandy

Taneesha

Taneisha

Tanela

Tanesa

Tanese

Tanesha

Taneshea

Taneshia

Tanesia

Tanessa

Tanessia

Taneta

Tanetta

Tangela

Tangi

Tangia

Tangie

Tanicha

Taniese

Taniesha

Tanika

Tanisa

Tanish

Tanisha

Tanishah

Tanishia

Tanissa

Tanita

Tanitha

Tanitia

Tanitra

Tanitta

Tanjia

Tanjie

Tannesa

Tannese

Tanneshia

Tannicia

Tanniece

Tanniecia

Tanniese

Tanniesha

Tannisa

Tannise

Tannisha

Tannus

Tannyce

Taquana

Taquanna

Taquera

Taquira

Tarsha

Tasha

Tashana

Tashanda

Tashani

Tashanna

Tashaonda

Tashauna

Tashawn

Tashawna

Tashay

Tashaya

Tashayla

Tashee

Tasheena

Tasheenah

Tasheeni

Tasheka

Tashell

Tashelle

Tashena

Tashenna

Tatianna

Tauna

Taunia

Taunisha

Tausha

Tawada

Tawana

Tawanda

Tawanna

Tawanne

Tawanza

Tawna

Tawnee

Tawnesha

Tawney

Tawni

Tawnia

Tawnya

Tayah

Tayana

Taye

Tayiah

Tayna

Tayra

Taysha

Tayshia

Taysia

Tayvonne

Teah

Teana

Teann

Teanna

Teanne

Teaunna

Techell

Techelle

Tedricka

Tee-ona

Teeiree

Teena

Teeona

Teeya

Tehanna

Teianna
Teina
Teishia
Teiya
Teja
Tejah
Tekeesha
Tekeisha
Telesia
Telicia
Telisa
Telisha
Telishia
Tellisa
Telma
Telsa
Temeka
Temequah
Temisha
Tempest
Tena
Tenae
Tenea
Tenecia
Teneesha
Tenehsa
Teneisha
Tenesha
Teneshia
Tenesia
Tenessa
Teneta
Tenetta
Tenezya
Tenice
Teniesha
Tenise

Tenisha
Tenishka
Tenita
Tenitta
Tennessa
Tenor
Teona
Tequana
Tequanna
Tequawna
Terena
Terita
Terria
Tesha
Teshell
Teshelle
Tetra
Teuana
Tewanna
Tewauna
Teyanna
Teyha
Teyona
Teyuna
Thea
Tia
Tiahna
Tiahni
Tiahnna
Tiaishia
Tiajuana
Tiamarie
Tiana
Tianda
Tiandra
Tiandria
Tianeka

Tianika
Tianna
Tiannah
Tiashauna
Tiauna
Tiawanna
Tiawna
Tiawni
Tiaya
Tiesha
Tieshia
Tiffani
Tiffany
Tihesha
Tijuana
Tikara
Tikesha
Tikia
Tikira
Tikisha
Tileta
Tilisha
Timaka
Timeeka
Timeka
Timesha
Timika
Timikia
Timisha
Tina
Tinesha
Tineshia
Tiniesha
Tinisha
Tinsia
Tionne
Tiquana

Tirika
Tisa
Tisha
Tishai
Tishan
Tishana
Tishani
Tishanna
Tishanne
Tishawn
Tishawna
Tisheena
Tishia
Tiwana
Tiwanah
Tiwanna
Tiya
Tiyah
Tiyana
Tiyanna
Tonda
Toneisha
Tonya
Toria
Toshanna
Toshauna
Toshawna
Towanda
Towanna
Tracia
Tralena
Tralyn
Tralynn
Tranesha
Tranice
Tranise
Trayana

Trayonna
Treiana
Treina
Tremell
Triana
Trianna
Trina
Trystal
Twana
Twyla
Tychell
Tychelle
Tyeisha
Tyesha
Tyisha
Tyleasha
Tyleisha
Tylena
Tylicia
Tylina
Tyline
Tylisha
Tylishia
Tymeka
Tymesha
Tymika
Tymmeeka
Tymmeka
Tyna
Tynelle
Tynesa
Tynesha
Tyneshia
Tynessa
Tyneta
Tynetta
Tynette

Tynice
Tyniese
Tyniesha
Tynise
Tynisha
Tyra
Tyrika
Tysa
Tysha
Tyshana
Tyshauna
Tyshawna
Tysheena
Tyshell
Tyshia
Tyshyna
Tyssa
Tywanda
Tywania
Tywanna

U
UniQue

V
Valencia
Valeria
Valerie
Valoris
Vaneisha
Vantrece
Vantrice
Velena
VeNay
Venita
Verise
Vernell

Vernessa
Vertise
Vona
Vonda
Vondra
Voneisha
Voneishia
Vonesha
Voneshia
Von'jai
Vonna
Vonni
Vonnie
Vonny
Vontricia
Vontriece

W
Wakesha
Wakeshia
Wakesia
Wanda
Wandalyn
Whitney
Wilma
Wyndolyn
Wynfred

X
Xada
Xaviera

Y
Yavonda
Yavonne
Yawna

Yentel
Yevette
Yolie
Yona
Yonette
Yvonne

Z
Zacceaus
Zahra
Zekia
Zelda
Zola

Boys

A
Aaron
Aathony
Adrian
Adric
Ahman
Akeem
Akiba
Akil
Alton
Aman
Amar
Amani
Amber
Amos
An-areal
Andre
Andreas
Andrew

Aneon
Antar
Antawn
Anterian
Anthone
Anthony
Antiere
Antiwan
Antoine
Antonio
Antowain
Antraevis
Antwan
Antwaun
Anwar
Ar'Keavius
Aray
Arcus
Arden
Aristis
Arlandus
Armstrong
Artavius
Aunda
Autry
Avery

B
Baakari
Baron
Barrington
Barry
Benjamin
Bernard
Bevaun
Bokeem

Booker
Bowe
Bowie
Braison
Brendon
Brockman
Budrow

C
Cadarius
Calbert
Calvin
Cameron
Canard
Carl
Carlester
Carnell
Carswell
Cartier
Casim
Cassius
Cavin
Cecil
Ceasar
Chalance
Chamas
Chante
Chantha
Chanthar
Chantra
Chidi
Chris
Christopher
Cicero
Cisqo
Clarence

Clayton
Cleavant
Cleavon
Clement
Clemon
Clendon
Clerrance
Clester
Cleveland
Clevon
Clifton
Clinton
Cody
Colin
Cook
Cordell
Cornelius
Cornell
Cornia
Curglin

D
D'andre
D'andrea
D'angelo
D'ante
D'anthony
D'juan
D'Lewis
D'lon
D'lonn
D'marco
D'marcus
D'Mark
D'marques
D'marreio

D'Ole
D'Sean
D'shaun
Da'quan
Da-Jon
Da-Juan
Da-Mar
Da-Shawn
Dacarlos
Daekwon
Daequan
Daevin
Deavon
Daiquan
Dajeon
Dajon
Dajuan
Dakeem
Dalen
Dallan
Dallen
Dallian
Dallin
Dallon
Dalton
Damarcius
Damarco
Damarius
Damon
Damone
Damontae
Danatay
Dandrae
Dandras
Dandray
Dandre

Dangelo
Dante
Dantereus
Danutaye
Danute
Daquain
Daquan
Daquann
Daquawn
Daqwan
Darel
Darell
Darik
Darian
Darius
Darnay
Darnel
Darrack
Darrian
Darroll
Darvenel
Daryl
Daryn
Dasan
Dasean
Dashaun
Dashawn
Dashon
Dassaun
Dauntay
Dauntrae
Davanté
Daven
Davian
Davin
Davinte

Davion
Davon
Davone
Davonn
Davonne
Davonte
Dawan
Dawaun
Dawawn
Dawin
Dawine
Dawon
Dawoyan
Dayquane
Dayton
Dayvon
De'andre
De'Angelo
De'kwan
De'Lewis
De'Lon
De'ron
De'shawn
De'vegas
De-Andre
De-Andrea
De-Angelo
De-Ante
De-Anthony
Dearse
De-Aundre
De-Carlos
De-John
De-Juan
De-Lewis
De-Marcus

De-Mario
De-Michael
De-rece
De-Ron
De-Sean
De-Wayne
Deandrae
Deandre
Deangleo
Deanglo
Deante
Deanthony
Deaundera
Deaundra
Deaundre
Deaundrey
Deaven
Decarlo
Decarlos
Dedrian
Deelon
Deherric
Deion
Deiven
DeJahn
Dejohn
Delane
Delante
Delaun
Dell
Delmar
Delmas
Delon
Delonn
Delroy
Demaine

Demarco	Deontevius	Devain
Demarcus	Deontia	Devaine
Demariee	Deontie	Deval
Demario	Deontre	Devale
Demarion	Deontrea	Devan
Demarius	Deontrez	Devane
Demarkes	Dequain	Devante
Demarkis	Dequan	Devaughn
Demarkus	Dequann	Devaunte
Demarius	Dequaun	Devayn
Demarreio	Dequion	Devayne
Demarrio	Dequon	Devein
Demerrio	Derick	Deveion
Demery	Dermonti	Deven
Demetrick	Deron	Devere
Demetrius	Derrick	Deverick
Demichael	Derrion	Devon
Demonde	Desean	Devondre
Demone	Deshan	Devonee
Demont	Deshane	Devonier
Demonte	Deshaun	Devonn
Demontez	Deshaune	Devonnaire
Demontre	Deshauwn	Devonta
Demoris	Deshawan	Devontae
Demorus	Deshawn	Devontate
Dennard	Deshay	Devontay
Denzel	Deshayne	Devonte
Deole	Deshea	Dewain
Deon	Deshon	Dewaine
Deondray	Deshondre	Dewalt
Deondre	Deshone	Dewan
Deonta	Deshonte	Dewayne
Deontae	Deshun	Dewon
Deontay	Desson	Dewune
Deonte	Detrich	Dexter
Deontee	Deuwayne	Deyonte

Di'angelo
Di'carlos
Diangelo
Diante
Dianthony
Dieondre
Dijuan
Diondre
Diontae
Diontay
Dionte
Dionus
Diron
Diuan
Dixon
Dmarco
Donall
Dondi
Dondrea
Dondres
Donell
Donnell
Donta
Dontae
Dontal
Dontao
Dontate
Dontay
Dontaye
Donte
Dontea
Dontee
Dontei
Donterius
Dontez

Dontrell
Dorsey
Dorshawn
Dovard
Draven
Dravius
Drayven
Drevon
Drewann
Duan
Duane
Dujuan
Dumonde
Duron
Dusean
Dushan
Dushaun
Dushawn
Duval
Dwaun
Dwaunn
Dwawn
Dwon
Dwuann
Dylan
Dyrell

E
Earvin
Eason
Eavin
Eddie
Eddrick
Edell
Edgerin

Edrick
Edward
Edwyn
Eldrick
Ellijahrell
Elton
Emme
Ennis
Enos
Erico
Ernard
Ernest
Erric
Ervan
Evander

F
Faheem
Farad
Fayard
Felleon
Fendrick
Ferric

G
Garcello
Garcene
Garlan
Garon
Garrick
Garrison
George
Gerain
Geroy
Glover

Godrell
Grant
Grayland
Gregory

H
Haile
Hareem
Hasan
Hasheem
Henry
Heran
Horace
Horus

I
Isiah
Ivory

J
J'Quan
J'Quez
Ja-ron
Jabar
Jabari
Jacoury
Jah'Quez
Jahquil
Jahvel
Jairus
Jalen
Jam'ih
Jamaar
Jamaari
Jamahrae

Jamal
Jamar
Jamara
Jamarco
Jamarcus
Jamari
Jamariel
Jamario
Jamarius
Jamarvis
Jamaur
Jamel
Jamele
Jamero
Jamir
Jamie
Jamison
Janeil
Jaquan
Jaquez
Jaquin
Jaquon
Jaqwan
Jared
Jarek
Jarel
Jarell
Jaric
Jarik
Jarious
Jarmar
Jarneil
Jarnell
Jarrick
Jarvis

Jason
Jauan
Jaumar
Ja'varis
Javon
Jawara
Jaykuam
Jayquan
Jayqwan
Je'rod
Jefferson
Jeffon
Jemaar
Jemar
Jemarcus
Jemario
Jemarus
Jenell
Jenuel
Jeraid
Jeremy
Jerick
Jerik
Jerimi
Jerin
Jermain
Jermaine
Jerohn
Jerom
Jerome
Jeron
Jerrick
Jessan
Jimar
Jimarcus

Jimmy

Jocez

John

Jonathon

Jorel

Jorell

Jorelle

Jorrel

Jorrell

Jovan

Julean

Juwan

Juwuane

K

Kadema

Kaheem

Kaleaf

Kamron

Kareen

Karson

Kasan

Kavon

Kaynard

Ke'Shawn

Ke-Andre

Ke-Sean

Ke-shawn

Ke-Shon

Keandrae

Keandre

Kearnice

Keenan

Keeshawn

Keiondre

Kenard

Kendell

Kendrick

Kennath

Kennlucky

Kenol

Kentata

Kenton

Kenyata

Keon

Keondre

Keontae

Keonte

Keontrye

Kerlin

Kesean

Keshaun

Keshawn

Keshon

Kevin

Keyon

Keyonte

Keyontre

Keshawn

Kieshun

Kimbel

Kiondre

Kireem

Kiyondre

Kleavon

Klevon

Kobe

Kordal

Kordell

Kwame

Kweisi

L

La'ron

La-corey

La-Ron

Lamair

Lamar

Lamaris

Lamarray

Lamont

Lance

Laquentin

Laquenton

Laquintas

Laquintin

Laquintiss

Laquinton

Laran

Larent

Larice

Larmar

Larnzell

Laron

Larone

Laronn

Larshun

Lasean

Lashawn

Lashon

Lashonne

Lashon

Latavious

Lateef

Lathan

Lathaniel

Lathe

Lathen
Lathyn
Latravis
Latrell
Latrivis
Lauana
Lavan
Lavaughan
Lavaughn
Lavernus
Lavon
Lavonne
Lawler
Lazarious
Le'Shon
Le-Quentin
Le-Ron
Le-Sean
Le-shon
Le-Vaughan
Lebaron
Ledell
Lee-Ron
Leeland
Leevon
Leguinn
Lemar
Lemario
Lemarr
Leon
Leondro
Lequentin
Lequenton
Lequinton
Leron
Lerone

Leroy
Lesean
Leshaun
Leshawn
Leshon
Lester
Levan
Levaughan
Levaughn
Levon
Levone
Levonn
Linwood
Liron
Lomus
Lott
Louis
Lovell
Lucius
Lumis
Luther
Lyndale

M
Makibe
Makques
Malcolm
Malik
Malsha
Mancel
Marcha
Marcus
Mariko
Markez
Maron
Marques

Marquez
Marquise
Martel
Marvus
Maurice
Medgar
Mekeda
Merlin
Meron
Merton
Messiah
Michael
Mikal
Milan
Mizell
Moises
Mont
Montavius
Montel
Montell
Montez
Monteze
Montisze
Montray
Montre
Montrell
Montres
Montrez
Mumia
Myles

N
Nafis
Nakia
Naquan
Natrick

Natron	Quinton	Rashun
Natrone	Quran	Raushan
Nelson		Raushawn
Noah	R	Raymone
Norrece	Rachard	Raymont
Nushan	Rachine	Raynard
	Radell	Rayquan
O	Radey	Raysan
O'Neil	Raequan	Raysean
Octavius	Raequon	Rayshaan
Odell	Rafiq	Rayshan
Omar	Raheem	Rayshaun
Omari	Rahmel	Rayshawn
Ondrey	Rahsean	Raysheen
Oniell	Rahul	Rayshon
Orlando	Rakeesh	Rayshone
Orpheus	Rakuan	Rayshun
Oteni	Ramell	Rayshunn
Othell	Randall	Reggie
Otis	Raquan	Reggis
	Rashaad	Regina
P	Rashaan	Reginald
Paeton	Rasham	Remus
Patrice	Rashan	Reshane
Pearson	Rashane	Reshaun
Phillip	Rashann	Reshaw
Primus	Rashard	Reshawn
Princeton	Rashaun	Reshay
	Rashaw	Reshean
Q	Rashawn	Resheen
Quadree	Rashean	Reshey
Quadrees	Rasheen	Reshon
Quentin	Rashien	Reshun
Quenton	Rashiena	Reynard
Quincy	Rashod	Rhashan
Quinteen	Rashon	Rhashaun

Rhashawn
Rishan
Rishaun
Rishawn
Rishon
Rodell
Rodney
Rohsaan
Rolandis
Romain
Romano
Romanos
Romario
Romayne
Rome
Romel
Romell
Romello
Romelo
Romeo
Romero
Romlo
Romman
Romolo
Romon
Romone
Ron-Dre
Rondale
Rondall
Ronde
Rondeal
Rondel
Rondell
Rondey
Rondie
Rondre

Rondrell
Rontae
Ronte
Rontez
Roscoe
Roshan
Roshane
Roshaun
Roshawn
Roshay
Roshean
Rosheen
Roshene
Roshon
Rufus
Rumaldo
Rydell

S
Sammy
Samuel
Santana
Saquan
Savion
Savoy
Sebastion
Senaca
Serek
Shadel
Shakeel
Shamaine
Shaman
Shamine
Shamon
Shamond
Shamondo

Shamone
Shan
Shane
Shandel
Shandon
Shandrel
Shango
Shant
Shantae
Shantay
Shante
Shantell
Shantelle
Shanti
Shanton
Shanty
Shaquille
Shaun
Shawnell
Shawnelle
Shawnta
Shawntae
Shawnte
Shawntel
Shawnti
Sheik
Sherman
Sherod
Sherwin
Shoaib
Shondae
Shondale
Shondel
Shonntay
Shontae
Shonte

Shyrod
Shyrone
Sidell
Simeon
Sorrell
Steadman
Sterlin
Stevie
Sylvester

T
Ta'Corian
Ta-Juan
Tabaris
Taejon
Taft
Taijon
Taijuan
Tailen
Tajuan
Tajwan
Talin
Tallon
Talon
Tamarick
Tamaurice
Tameron
Taquan
Taras
Tarek
Taron
Tarus
Tashai
Taunt
Tauraus
Tavares

Tavion
Tavis
Taye
Taylan
Taylen
Tayshawn
Teance
Tenard
Terell
Terris
Theodor
Theron
Tiyshan
Tobiaus
Toborrious
Toussaint
Tramaine
Travahn
Travanis
Travante
Travaugh
Travon
Travonn
Travonne
Tre'jon
Tre'Vaughn
Trece
Trejean
Tremaine
Trenton
Treshaun
Tresis
Trevaun
Treven
Trevin
Trevon

Trevone
Tupac
Turell
Tyree
Tyreek
Tyreese
Tyreik
Tyrek
Tyreke
Tyrell
Tyrese
Tyric
Tyrick
Tyriek
Tyrik
Tyriq
Tyrique
Tyronne
Tyrus
Tyshaun
Tyshawn
Tyvin
Tywan

U
Umar

V
Vance
Vashae
Vashan
Vashann
Vashaun
Vashawn
Vashon
Vaugn

Vennis
Vishon

W
Wardell
Warwick
Waverly
Wayan
Wendell
Wesley
Wilburn

Willie
Winton
Wyclef
Wyton

X
Xavier

Y
Yemar
Yusef

Z
Zachary
Zchon
Zeshan
Zeshaun
Zeshawn
Zeshon

Bibliography

Algotsson, Sharne, and Dennys Davis. *The Spirit of African Design.* New York: Random House, 1996.

Bastide, Roger. *African Civilizations in the New World.* New York: Harper and Row, 1971.

Beasley, Donna, and Donna Carter. *Family Pride: The Complete Guide to Tracing African-American Genealogy.* Foster City, CA: IDG Books Worldwide, 1997.

Cole, Harriette. *Jumping the Broom.* New York: Henry Holt and Company, 1995.

Felder, Rev. Cain Hope, ed. *The Original African Heritage Study Bible: King James Version.* Nashville, TN: James C. Winston Publishing Company, 1996.

Gottlieb, Alma. *Culture and Infancy in Africa.* Urbana: University of Illinois, 1995.

Kilbride, Janet C., and Philip L. Kilbride. *Changing Family Life in East Africa: Women at Risk.* University Park: Pennsylvania State University Press, 1990.

Kudajie, Joshua. *African Proverbs: Collections, Studies, Bibliographies.* Colorado Springs, CO: Global Mapping International, 1996.

Leslau, Charlotte, and Wolf Leslau. *African Proverbs.* New York: Peter Pauper Press, 1985.

LeVine, Sarah. *Mothers and Wives.* Chicago, IL: University of Chicago Press, 1979.

McKnight, Reginald, ed. *The Wisdom of the African World.* Novato, CA: Classic Wisdom Collection, 1996.

Mbiti, John S. *African Religions and Philosophy.* New York: Praeger, 1969.
———. *The Role of Women in Traditional African Religion.* New York: Praeger, 1969.

Mfume, Kweisi. *No Free Ride.* New York: Ballantine Books, 1996.

Ottenberg, Simon, and Phoebe Ottenberg, eds. *Cultures and Societies of Africa.* New York: Random House, 1960.

Wiggins, William H., Jr., and Douglas DeNatale. *Jubilation! African-American Celebrations in the Southeast.* Columbia: University of South Carolina, 1993.

Williamson, Suzanne. *Entertaining for Dummies.* Foster City, CA: IDG Books Worldwide, 1997.

Tell Us Your Story

About your pregnancy, baby shower, or naming ceremony. It may be used in future revisions or for an entirely new book. Send your story to:

Pocket Books
1230 Avenue of the Americas
New York, NY 10020
Attn: Janice Robinson, Author

Index

Abarry, Dr. Abu, 36
Adinkra cloth symbols, 52, 76–77
adopted child, baby shower for, 43–44
adult naming ceremonies, 129–33
Afoakwa Mpoankron, 76
African-American baby shower:
    activities for adult guests, 58–62, 66
    activities for children and siblings at, 62–64
    for adopted child, 43–44
    centerpieces for, 53–55
    decor, 52–53
    differences from Afrocentric shower, 35
    guest list preparation, 47–48
    honoring the wishes of mother-to-be, 39
    hosting, 38
    invitations for, 47–51
    length of, 37
    location of, 37–38
    long-distance, 40
    party favors for, 56–58
    planning, 35–66
    recipes for, 27–33
    surprise, 47–48
    themes for, 46, 65–66
    timeline for planning, 39–40
    timing of, 35–37
    types of, 41–46
African-American Kitchen (Medearis), 25
African Caribbean Dance Theatre, Inc., 6
African doll and animal centerpieces, 55–56
African fertility dolls centerpiece, 54
African naming ceremonies, 125–27
African sand art, 62, 83
Afrocentric baby shower, 3–12
    customs associated with, 3–4
    dancing and drumming, 5–6
    host's role, 4
    menu for, 26

    musical suggestions for, 6
    party themes, 7–13
    storytelling at, 6–7
    timing of, 3–4
Afrocentric patterns, 147
Akamban customs and proverbs, 83, 84, 95
alcoholic beverages:
    libations, 10
    during pregnancy, 10
American Greetings Company, 26
Aro of Sierra Leone, prayer of, 17
Ashanti customs and proverbs, 3, 17, 83, 87, 97, 100, 125
Ashanti stools, 71–72
Australian naming ceremonies, 102
Azande customs, 94

Baby-Bath Punch, 25
Baby Beef Barbecue Ribs, 27–28
baby block scrabble, 60
Baby Bottle centerpiece, 53
baby bracelets, making, 64
Baby Carriage Fruit Basket, 29–30
baby lottery game, 59
baby pictures of guests, game using, 60–61
baby on a plate game, 61
baby-proofing kits, 73
baby showers:
    African-American. *See* African-American baby
        shower.
    with African-American theme, xx
    Afrocentric. *See* Afrocentric baby shower.
    food for. *See* food for baby showers.
    planning, 35–66
    religious elements in, 15–19
    as rites of passage, xix
    timing of, 3–4, 35–37
balaphone, 116
balloons, 55

Bambuti customs, 85
Banyarwanda customs, 94
baptism, xx, 100, 102
barbecues, 26
Barotse prayer, 18
"basket names," 92
bath and body party favors, 57
Beef Barbecue Ribs, Baby, 27–28
beer libations, 10
benediction, closing, 18, 116
beverages, 23–25
    Baby-Bath Punch, 25
    bissap juice, 121
    Sherbet Punch, 25
Bible verses about children and parents, 114
birth announcements, 18–19
birth customs and rituals, 81–88
Black Storytellers Alliance, 7
blankets. See quilts.
blessings. See prayers and blessings.
block prints, Afrocentric, 77
books:
    cookbooks, African-American, 25
    as gifts, 43, 72–73, 79
    to research ancestral names, 95–96
bubbles, 64
Bundt cake and baby bottle, 23
Burundi customs, 84, 94

cake for baby shower, 22–23
    Bundt cake with baby bottle, 23
    decorating with words, 24
    Swahili Baby-Block Cake, 23
calabash bowl, 31, 117, 121
cameras for children, 43
candle lighting at naming ceremony, 113, 115
Catholic ceremonies, 102
centerpieces:
    for baby shower, 53–55
    for naming ceremony, 117–18
Chicken:
    Senegalese Yassa, 119–20
    Wingettes, Kickin', 27
chocolate bars, party favor, 57–58
Christian confirmation ceremony, 102
cider libations, 10
cleaning up, 19, 33
closing benediction, 18–19, 116
commemorative birth plate, 73
community journal, 11
community quilt, 12–13

computers:
    cyber shower, 41
    invitations made on, 50
confirmation, 102
cookbooks, African-American, 25
Cornbread, Mealy, 123
corsage, wrapping paper, 53
couple baby shower, 46
Cous-Cous, Tunisian Vegetable, 120–21
cowry shells, 53, 71
crab feast, 26
creative baby shower, 46
cyber shower, 41

dads:
    gifts for, 72
    gifts from, 68
    shower for, 44–46
Daffo-Batura customs, 126
dancing, African, xviii–xix, 5–6
decor for African-American baby shower, 52–53
Diaper Cake centerpiece, 54
Didinga customs, 85
Dimensions Dance Theater, 5–6
dirty diaper pin game, 62
Djoniba Dance & Drum Centre, 5
double shower, 44
drumming, African, 5–6
Duckitt, Hildagonda, 25

Eggs, Lil' Angel, 28
etiquette tips, 12, 19, 33, 65–66, 79

Fanti customs, 70, 87, 97, 100
fathers. See dads.
finger food and hors d'oeuvres, 25–26
fish fry, 26
food for baby showers, 21–33
    Afrocentric menu, 26
    beverages, 23–25
    cake, 21–23
    finger food and hors d'oeuvres, 25–26
    prayers of thanks, 18
    recipes. See recipes for African-American baby
        shower.
Food Lover's Companion, The (Herbst), 25
food for naming ceremonies, 117–23
    gifts of, 117
    menu, 118–19
    recipes, 119–23
Fulani people of Sudan, customs and proverbs of, 38, 85–86

games for baby showers, 58–62
Ghana, customs and proverbs of, 49, 67, 70, 81, 83–84, 117
gifts, 36, 67–79
    African, common and traditional, 70
    Afrocentric, 75
    books as, 43, 72–73, 79
    from dads, 68
    for dad's shower, 45
    etiquette, 66, 79
    of food, 117
    from godparents, 79
    ideas for, 69–75
    naming ceremony, 105, 111
    naming ceremony for adult, 132
    prayer of thanks, 17
    registries, 51, 66, 68–69, 79
    for second, third, or fourth baby shower, 42
    for siblings, 42–43
    time for opening, 17
    wrappings, Afrocentric, 75–77
Giyuku customs, 85, 87–88
goatskin drum, 116
godparents, xx, 77–79
goody bag, mom's, 70–71
grand bubah, 104
griot, 107–08
guest list for African-American baby shower, 47–48

hair shaving, ritual:
    of baby at naming ceremony, 108–09
    of mother after birth, 87–88
hat, paper-plate, 53
healthy cooking, 120
Healthy Soul Food Cookbook, The (Jones), 25
herbal tea party favors, 58
Herbst, Sharon Tyler, 25
heritage quilts, 70
hors d'oeuvres and finger food, 25–26
host:
    of African-American baby shower, 38
    of Afrocentric baby shower, 4
Hot Plantain Chips, 32

Ibo naming ceremony, 127
India, naming ceremonies in, 102
Ingassana customs, 85
International Star Registry, 94
invitations, 66
    Afrocentric patterns for, 147
    baby shower, 47–51

    information to include, 51
    to naming ceremonies, 104

Jewish naming ceremonies, 101
Jones, Wilbert, 25
journal, community, 11

karaoke momma game, 60
Kemetic symbols from Egypt, 52, 92, 93
Kente cloth, 52, 66, 70, 76
Kenyan customs and proverbs, 67
    eggs as party favors, 57
Khalidah's North Afrikan Dance Experience, 5
Khasi naming ceremony, 126
Kickin' Chicken Wingettes, 27
kids say the darnedest things, 63
Kola Nuts, 121
kora, 107, 116
Koran, verses about children and parents from the, 114
kufi, 104
Kwanzaa promise, 8
Kwanzaa shower, 7–8
Kweisi Mfume, 130

libations, 9–10
    at naming ceremony, 111
    prayers, 9, 83–84, 112
Lil' Angel Eggs, 28
Lil' Sweet Pea Salad, 29
long-distance baby shower, 39–40
lottery game, baby, 59
Lozi proverb, 117

Macaroni and Sweet Pea Salad, 29
Malcolm X, 129
Mamatoto, 4
Mandinka customs, 94, 113
Mao customs, 85
marker mania activity, 64
Masai customs and proverbs, 16, 84
Mbiti, John S., 94
meals. See food for baby showers; food for naming ceremonies.
Mealy Cornbread, 123
Medearis, Angela Shelf, 25
menu:
    for Afrocentric baby shower, 26
    naming ceremony, 118–19
milk libations, 10
modeling clay, 64
Molefi Kete Asante, 130–31

Moroccan Spiced Olives, 33
mother-of-honor chair, 52–53
music, 6, 65, 116

name change:
    adult naming ceremonies, 129–33
    legal, procedure for, 133
naming ceremonies, 89–133
    African attire for, 104
    African ceremonies, 125–27
    announcing of selected names at, 112
    the benediction, 116
    centerpieces, 117–18
    ceremonial and symbolic items at, 105–07
    death of child prior to, 95
    entertainment for, 104
    gifts for, 105, 111, 132
    the griot at, 107–08
    inviting guests, 104
    the libation at, 111
    lighting of central candle, 113
    lighting of the ceremonial candles, 115
    location for, 103, 104
    menu, 118–19
    officiant at, 111
    for older folks, 129–33
    the orations, 115
    in other cultures and groups, 101–02
    preparation for, 103–09
    presentation of the child, 115
    presenting the ceremonial items, 113
    procession, 108
    purpose of, xx
    recipes for, 119–23
    rites, 111–16
    as rites of passage, xix
    ritual cleansing before, 108
    shaving baby's hair at, 108–09
    significance of, xx
    the symbolic first step, 113
    timing of, 103
    traditional, 99–102
    Unity Cup, 112
naming a child:
    African names, 96–97
    ancestral names, researching, 95–96
    Black American names, 98
    boys' names, popular urban, 166–77
    day of birth and, 97
    girls' names, popular urban, 149–66
    heaven, African names from, 96–97

    incorporating God's name in child's name, 94
    multiple names, 100
    responsibility for naming the child, 93
    royal families, African names reserved for, 97
    selecting an Afrocentric name, 94–96
    significance of a name, xix, 91–93
    in slavery, xv, 91–92, 100
    time for, 93
Native American naming ceremonies, 101
Ndebele customs, 85
Nepalese naming ceremonies, 102
Nigerian naming ceremony, 126
Nigerian proverb, 135
Niger naming ceremony, 126
Nuer people, customs and proverbs of, 17–18, 94

Ogunfiditimi, Reverend Fred, 92
Okra and Tomatoes, Stewed, 122–23
Old Wives' Tall Tales, 58–59
Olives, Moroccan Spiced, 33

party favors, 56–58
    Afrocentric patterns for, 147
photographs:
    etiquette tips, 12, 19
picture frames as party favors, 58
pin the baby on the new mom, 61
Plantain Chips, Hot, 32
plants as centerpieces, 55
play-doh, 64
pocketbook peek-a-boo game, 61
poem for African naming ceremony, 115
porridge, 32
Poussaint, Dr. Alvin F., xiii–xv
prayers and blessings, 83–84
    during baby showers, 15–18
    closing benediction, 18–19, 116
    libation, 9, 83–84, 112
    at naming ceremony, 112, 113
    videotaping guests', 62
pregnancy:
    African customs, 84–85
    alcoholic beverages during, 10
    cravings during, 33
    spiritual meaning of, 3, 36
    taboos, 36
pregnancy pictionary, 62
price is right game, 61
proverbs, African:
    decorating cake with, 24
    for invitations, 50, 51

See also individual countries and people.
Pygmy customs, 113

quilts:
community, 12–13
heritage, 70

Randall, Joe, 25
recipes:
for African-American baby shower, 27–33
Barbecue Ribs, Baby Beef, 27–28
Chicken, Senegalese Yassa, 119–20
Chicken Wingettes, Kickin', 27
Cornbread, Mealy, 122–23
Cous-Cous, Tunisian Vegetable, 120–21
Eggs, Lil' Angel, 28
healthy cooking tips, 120
Kola Nuts, 121
for naming ceremony, 119–23
Okra and Tomatoes, Stewed, 122–23
Olives, Moroccan Spiced, 33
Plantain Chips, Hot, 32
Sweet Pea Salad, Lil', 29
Sweet Potato Pie, 122
registries for gifts, 51, 66, 68–69, 79
religious elements at baby shower, 15–19
religious verses about children and parents, 114
resource guide, 135–45
restaurants, showers at, 65
Ribs, Baby Beef Barbecue, 27–28
ritual cleansing before naming ceremony, 108
ritual closing for Afrocentric shower, 13
Roots, xix

sacrificial goat or sheep, 87, 118
salad:
Fruit Basket, Baby Carriage, 29–30
salad bar, 31
Sweet Pea, Lil', 29
sand and water table, 64
second or later child, shower for, 41–43
Senegalese customs, xviii, 108
Senegalese sand art, 62, 83
Senegalese tea, 121
Shangana customs, 86
shaving of hair, ritual:
baby's, at naming ceremony, 108–09
mother's, after birth, 87–88
Sherbet Punch, 25
shoes, removal of, 4
siblings:

activities at baby shower for, 62–64
gifts for, 42–43
inviting, 48
Sierra Leone saying, 103
sister-circle, 11, 13
slavery, naming of children in, xv, 91–92, 100
Somalian customs and proverbs, 3–4, 36, 125–26
soul food, origin of expression, 25
South African customs and proverbs, 4
storytelling, African, 6–7
strawberry wine libations, 10
surprise baby shower, 47–48
Swahili Baby-Block Cake, 23
Sweet Pea Salad, Lil', 29
Sweet Potato Pie, 122
symbols:
Adinkra cloth, 52, 76–77
Kemetic, 52, 92, 93
at naming ceremony, 105–07, 113

taboos:
pregnancy, 36, 84–85, 87, 88
timing of baby showers and, 3–4
Tanzanian proverbs, 89
tap dancing, 5
Taste of Heritage, A (Randall and Martin), 25
tea:
herbal tea party favors, 58
Senegalese, 121
tea party, 64
teddy bear and African doll centerpieces, 55–56
thank-you notes, 18, 19
themes:
African-American baby showers, 46, 65–66
Afrocentric shower, 7–13
time capsule, baby's, 69
timeline for planning baby shower, 39–40
Tipton-Martin, Toni, 25
toilet paper measure game, 61
Tomatoes and Okra, Stewed, 122–23
Traditional South African Cookery (Duckitt), 25
travel bag, baby, 70
trust walk, 11
T-shirt art, 59–60
Tsonga customs, 86
twins, baby shower for, 44

Udhuk customs, 85
Umoja Karamu shower, 8–9
Unity Cup, 112

videotaping:
    children at baby shower, 63
    guest blessings, 62

washing dishes, 33
water libations, 10
Watermelon Baby Carriage Fruit Basket, 29–30
West African customs and proverbs, 36
Wolof customs, 85, 86, 127
wrapping gifts Afrocentrically, 75–77
wrapping paper corsage, 53

yams, 122
Yansi customs, 85
Yoruban customs and proverbs, 15, 93, 94, 103, 107

Zairean proverb, 129
Zambian customs and proverbs, 21
Zimbabwe customs, 73
Zulu customs and proverbs, 4